THE STORY OF
TROY

MICHAEL CLARKE

The Story of Troy

Michael Clarke

© 1st World Library, 2007
PO Box 2211
Fairfield, IA 52556
www.1stworldlibrary.com
First Edition

LCCN: 2007901833

Softcover ISBN: 978-1-4218-4305-6
Hardcover ISBN: 978-1-4218-4207-3
eBook ISBN: 978-1-4218-4403-9

Purchase *"The Story of Troy"*
as a traditional bound book at:
www.1stWorldLibrary.com/purchase.asp?ISBN=978-1-4218-4305-6

1st World Library is a literary, educational organization
dedicated to:

- Creating a free internet library of downloadable ebooks

- Hosting writing competitions and offering book publishing
  scholarships.

Interested in more 1st World Library books? contact:
literacy@1stworldlibrary.com
Check us out at: www.1stworldlibrary.com

1st World Library Literary Society

Giving Back to the World

"If you want to work on the core problem, it's early school literacy."

- James Barksdale, former CEO of Netscape

"No skill is more crucial to the future of a child, or to a democratic and prosperous society, than literacy."

- Los Angeles Times

"Literacy... means far more than learning how to read and write... The aim is to transmit... knowledge and promote social participation."

- UNESCO

"Literacy is not a luxury, it is a right and a responsibility. If our world is to meet the challenges of the twenty-first century we must harness the energy and creativity of all our citizens."

- President Bill Clinton

"Parents should be encouraged to read to their children, and teachers should be equipped with all available techniques for teaching literacy, so the varying needs and capacities of individual kids can be taken into account."

- Hugh Mackay

CONTENTS

INTRODUCTION

I. HOMER, THE FATHER OF POETRY.

In this book we are to tell the story of Troy, and particularly of the famous siege which ended in the total destruction of that renowned city. It is a story of brave warriors and heroes of 3000 years ago, about whose exploits the greatest poets and historians of ancient times have written. Some of the wonderful events of the memorable siege are related in a celebrated poem called the Il'i-ad, written in the Greek language. The author of this poem was Ho'mer, who was the author of another great poem, the Od'ys-sey, which tells of the voyages and adventures of the Greek hero, U-lys'ses, after the taking of Troy.

Homer has been called the Father of Poetry, because he was the first and greatest of poets. He lived so long ago that very little is known about him. We do not even know for a certainty when or where he was born. It is believed, however, that he lived in the ninth century before Christ, and that his native place was Smyr'na, in Asia Minor. But long after his death several other cities claimed the honor of being his birthplace.

Seven Grecian cities vied for Homer dead,
Through which the living Homer begged his bread.

LEONIDAS.

It is perhaps not true that Homer was so poor as to be obliged to beg for his bread; but it is probable that he earned his living by traveling from city to city through many parts of Greece and Asia Minor, reciting his poems in the palaces of princes, and at public assemblies. This was one of the customs of ancient times, when the art of writing was either not known, or very little practiced. The poets, or bards, of those days committed their compositions to memory, and repeated them aloud at gatherings of the people, particularly at festivals and athletic games, of which the ancient Greeks were very fond. At those games prizes and rewards were given to the bards as well as to the athletes.

It is said that in the latter part of his life the great poet became blind, and that this was why he received the name of Homer, which signified a blind person. The name first given to him, we are told, was Mel-e-sig'e-nes, from the river Me'les, a small stream on the banks of which his native city of Smyrna was situated.

So little being known of Homer's life, there has been much difference of opinion about him among learned men. Many have believed that Homer never existed. Others have thought that the Iliad and Odyssey were composed not by one author, but by several. "Some," says the English poet, Walter Savage Landor, "tell us that there were twenty Homers, some deny that there was ever one." Those who believe that there were "twenty Homers" think that different parts of the two great poems—the Iliad and Odyssey—were composed by different persons, and that all the parts were afterwards put together in the form in which they now appear. The opinion of most scholars at present, however, is that Homer did really exist, that he was a wandering bard, or minstrel, who sang or recited verses or ballads composed by himself, about the great deeds of heroes and warriors, and that those ballads,

Michael Clarke

collected and arranged in after years in two separate books, form the poems known as the Iliad and Odyssey.

Homer's poetry is what is called epic poetry, that is, it tells about heroes and heroic actions. The Iliad and Odyssey are the first and greatest of epic poems. In all ages since Homer's time, scholars have agreed in declaring them to be the finest poetic productions of human genius. No nation in the world has ever produced poems so beautiful or so perfect. They have been read and admired by learned men for more than 2000 years. They have been translated into the languages of all civilized countries. In this book we make many quotations from the fine translation of the Iliad by our American poet, William Cullen Bryant. We quote also from the well-known translation by the English poet, Alexander Pope.

The ancients had a very great admiration for the poetry of Homer. We are told that every educated Greek could repeat from memory any passage in the Iliad or Odyssey. Alexander the Great was so fond of Homer's poems that he always had them under his pillow while he slept. He kept the Iliad in a richly ornamented casket, saying that "the most perfect work of human genius ought to be preserved in a box the most valuable and precious in the world."

So great was the veneration the Greeks had for Homer, that they erected temples and altars to him, and worshiped him as a god. They held festivals in his honor, and made medals bearing the figure of the poet sitting on a throne and holding in his hands the Iliad and Odyssey. One of the kings of E'gypt built in that country a magnificent temple, in which was set up a statue of Homer, surrounded with a beautiful representation of the seven cities that contended for the honor of being the place of his birth.

Great bard of Greece, whose ever-during verse

All ages venerate, all tongues rehearse;
Could blind idolatry be justly paid
To aught of mental power by man display'd,
To thee, thou sire of soul-exalting song,
That boundless worship might to thee belong.

HAYLEY.

Michael Clarke

II. THE GODS AND GODDESSES.

To understand the Story of Troy it is necessary to know something about the gods and goddesses, who played so important a part in the events we are to relate. We shall see that in the Tro'jan War nearly everything was ordered or directed by a god or goddess. The gods, indeed, had much to do in the causing of the war, and they took sides in the great struggle, some of them helping the Greeks and some helping the Trojans.

The ancient Greeks believed that there were a great many gods. According to their religion all parts of the universe,— the heavens and the earth, the sun and the moon, the ocean, seas, and rivers, the mountains and forests, the winds and storms,—were ruled by different gods. The gods, too, it was supposed, controlled all the affairs of human life. There were a god of war and a god of peace, and gods of music, and poetry, and dancing, and hunting, and of all the other arts or occupations in which men engaged.

The gods, it was believed, were in some respects like human beings. In form they usually appeared as men and women. They were passionate and vindictive, and often quarreled among themselves. They married and had children, and needed food and drink and sleep. Sometimes they married human beings, and the sons of such marriages were the heroes of antiquity, men of giant strength who performed daring and wonderful feats. The food of the gods was Am-bro'sia, which conferred immortality and perpetual youth on those who partook of it; their drink was a delicious wine called Nec'tar.

The gods, then, were immortal beings. They never died; they never grew old, and they possessed immense power. They could change themselves, or human beings, into any form, and they could make themselves visible or invisible at pleasure. They could travel through the skies, or over earth or ocean, with the rapidity of lightning, often riding in gorgeous golden chariots drawn by horses of immortal breed. They were greatly feared by men, and when any disaster occurred,—if lives were lost by earthquake, or shipwreck, or any other calamity,—it was attributed to the anger of some god.

Though immortal beings, however, the gods were subject to some of the physical infirmities of humanity. They could not die, but they might be wounded and suffer bodily pain the same as men. They often took part in the quarrels and wars of people on earth, and they had weapons and armor like human warriors.

The usual place of residence of the principal gods was on the top of Mount O-lym'pus in Greece. Here they dwelt in golden palaces, and they had a Council Chamber where they frequently feasted together at grand banquets, celestial music being rendered by A-pol'lo, the god of minstrelsy, and the Muses, who were the divinities of poetry and song.

In all the chief cities grand temples were erected for the worship of the gods. One of the most famous was the Par'the-non, at Athens. At the shrines of the gods costly gifts in gold and silver were presented, and on their altars, often built in the open air, beasts were killed and burned as sacrifices, which were thought to be very pleasing to the divine beings to whom they were offered.

The greatest and most powerful of the gods was Ju'pi-ter, also called Jove or Zeus. To him all the rest were subject. He was the king of the gods, the mighty Thunderer, at whose nod Olympus shook, and at whose word the heavens trembled. From his great power in the regions of the sky he was sometimes called the "cloud-compelling Jove."

Michael Clarke

He, whose all-conscious eyes the world behold,
The eternal Thunderer sat, enthroned in gold.
High heaven the footstool of his feet he makes,
And wide beneath him all Olympus shakes.

POPE, *Iliad*, Book VIII.

The wife of Jupiter, and the queen of heaven, was Ju'no, who, as we shall see, was the great enemy of Troy and the Trojans. One of the daughters of Jupiter, called Ve'nus, or Aph-ro-di'te, was the goddess of beauty and love. Nep'tune was the god of the sea. He usually carried in his hand a trident, or three-pronged scepter, the emblem of his authority.

His sumptuous palace-halls were built
Deep down in ocean, golden, glittering, proof
Against decay of time.

BRYANT, *Iliad*, Book XIII.

Mars was the god of war, and Plu'to, also called Dis and Ha'des, was god of the regions of the dead. One of the most glorious and powerful of the gods was Apollo, or Phœ'bus, or Smin'theus, for he had many names. He was god of the sun, and of medicine, music, and poetry. He is represented as holding in his hand a bow, and sometimes a lyre. Homer calls him the "god of the silver bow," and the "far-darting Apollo," for the ancients believed that with the dart of his arrow he sent down plagues upon men whenever they offended him.

The other principal deities mentioned by Homer are Mi-ner'va, or Pal'las, the goddess of wisdom; Vul'can, the god of fire; and Mer'cu-ry, or Her'mes, the messenger of Jupiter. Vulcan was also the patron, or god, of smiths. He had several forges; one was on Mount Olympus, and another was supposed to be under Mount Æt'na in Sic'i-ly. Here, with his giant workmen, the Cy'clops, he made thunderbolts for Jupiter, and sometimes armor and weapons of war for earthly heroes.

The gods, it was believed, made their will known to men in various ways,—sometimes by the flight of birds, frequently by dreams, and sometimes by appearing on earth under different forms, and speaking directly to kings and warriors. Very often men learned the will of the gods by consulting seers and soothsayers, or augurs,—persons who were supposed to have the power of foretelling events. There were temples also where the gods gave answers through priests. Such answers were called Or'a-cles, and this name was also given to the priests. The most celebrated oracle of ancient times was in the temple of Apollo at Del'phi, in Greece. To this place people came from all parts of the world to consult the god, whose answers were given by a priestess called Pyth'i-a.

The ancients never engaged in war or any other important undertaking without sacrificing to the gods or consulting their oracles or soothsayers. Before going to battle they made sacrifices to the gods. If they were defeated in battle they regarded it as a sign of the anger of Jupiter, or Juno, or Minerva, or Apollo, or some of the other great beings who dwelt on Olympus. When making leagues or treaties of peace, they called the gods as witnesses, and prayed to Father Jupiter to send terrible punishments on any who should take false oaths, or break their promises. In the story of the Trojan War we shall find many examples of such appeals to the gods by the chiefs on both sides.

"O Father Jove, who rulest from the top
Of Ida, mightiest one and most august!
Whichever of these twain has done the wrong,
Grant that he pass to Pluto's dwelling, slain,

While friendship and a faithful league are ours.

"O Jupiter most mighty and august!
Whoever first shall break these solemn oaths,
So may their brains flow down upon the earth,—
Theirs and their children's."

BRYANT, *Iliad*, Book III.

I. TROY BEFORE THE SIEGE

That part of Asia Minor which borders the narrow channel now known as the Dar-da-nelles', was in ancient times called Tro'as. Its capital was the city of Troy, which stood about three miles from the shore of the Æ-ge'an Sea, at the foot of Mount Ida, near the junction of two rivers, the Sim'o-is, and the Sca-man'der or Xan'thus. The people of Troy and Troas were called Trojans.

Some of the first settlers in northwestern Asia Minor, before it was called Troas, came from Thrace, a country lying to the north of Greece. The king of these Thra'cian colonists was Teu'cer. During his reign a prince named Dar'danus arrived in the new settlement. He was a son of Jupiter, and he came from Sam'o-thrace, one of the many islands of the Ægean Sea. It is said that he escaped from a great flood which swept over his native island, and that he was carried on a raft of wood to the coast of the kingdom of Teucer. Soon afterwards he married Teucer's daughter. He then built a city for himself amongst the hills of Mount Ida, and called it Dar-da'ni-a; and on the death of Teucer he became king of the whole country, to which he gave the same name, Dardania.

> Jove was the father, cloud-compelling Jove,
> Of Dardanus, by whom Dardania first
> Was peopled, ere our sacred Troy was built
> On the great plain,—a populous town; for men

Michael Clarke

Dwelt still upon the roots of Ida fresh
With Qiany springs.

BRYANT, *Iliad*, Book XX.

Dardanus was the ancestor of the Trojan line of kings. He had a grandson named Tros, and from him the city Troy, as well as the country Troas, took its name. The successor of King Tros was his son I'lus. By him Troy was built, and it was therefore also called Il'i-um or Il'i-on; hence the title of Homer's great poem,—the Iliad. From the names Dardanus and Teucer the city of Troy has also been sometimes called Dardania and Teu'cri-a, and the Trojans are often referred to as Dardanians and Teucrians. Ilus was succeeded by his son La-om'e-don, and Laomedon's son Pri'am was king of Troy during the famous siege.

The story of the founding of Troy is a very interesting one. Ilus went forth from his father's city of Dardania, in search of adventures, as was the custom of young princes and heroes in those days; and he traveled on until he arrived at the court of the king of Phryg'i-a, a country lying east of Troas. Here he found the people engaged in athletic games, at which the king gave valuable prizes for competition. Ilus took part in a wrestling match, and he won fifty young men and fifty maidens,—a strange sort of prize we may well think, but not at all strange or unusual in ancient times, when there were many slaves everywhere. During his stay in Phrygia the young Dardanian prince was hospitably entertained at the royal palace. When he was about to depart, the king gave him a spotted heifer, telling him to follow the animal, and to build a city for himself at the place where she should first lie down to rest.

Ilus did as he was directed. With his fifty youths and fifty maidens he set out to follow the heifer, leaving her free to go along at her pleasure. She marched on for many miles, and at last lay down at the foot of Mount Ida on a beautiful plain watered by two rivers, and here Ilus encamped for the night. Before going to sleep he prayed to Jupiter to send him a sign that that was the site meant for his city. In the morning he found standing in front of his tent a wooden statue of the goddess Minerva, also called Pallas. The figure was three cubits high. In its right hand it held a spear, and in the left, a distaff and spindle.

This was the Pal-la'di-um of Troy, which afterwards became very famous. The Trojans believed that it had been sent down from heaven, and that the safety of their city depended upon its preservation. Hence it was guarded with the greatest care in a temple specially built for the purpose.

Ilus, being satisfied that the statue was the sign for which he had prayed, immediately set about building his city, and thus Troy was founded. It soon became the capital of Troas and the richest and most powerful city in that part of the world. During the reign of Laomedon, son of Ilus, its mighty walls were erected, which in the next reign withstood for ten years all the assaults of the Greeks. These walls were the work of no human hands. They were built by the ocean god Neptune. This god had conspired against Jupiter and attempted to dethrone him, and, as a punishment, his kingdom of the sea was taken away from him for one year, and he was ordered to spend that time in the service of the king of Troy.

In building the great walls, Neptune was assisted by Apollo, who had also been driven from Olympus for an offense against Jupiter. Apollo had a son named Æs-cu-la'pi-us, who was so skilled a physician that he could, and did, raise people from death to life. Jupiter was very angry at this. He feared that men might forget him and worship Æsculapius. He therefore hurled a thunderbolt at the great physician and killed him. Enraged at the death of his son, Apollo threatened to destroy the Cyclops, the giant workmen of

Vulcan, who had forged the terrible thunderbolt. Before he could carry out his threat, however, Jupiter expelled him from heaven. He remained on earth for several years, after which he was permitted to return to his place among the gods on the top of Mount Olympus.

Though Neptune was bound to serve Laomedon for one year, there was an agreement between them that the god should get a certain reward for building the walls. But when the work was finished the Trojan king refused to keep his part of the bargain. Apollo had assisted by his powers of music. He played such tunes that he charmed even the huge blocks of stone, so that they moved themselves into their proper places, after Neptune had wrenched them from the mountain sides and had hewn them into shape. Moreover, Apollo had taken care of Laomedon's numerous flocks on Mount Ida. During the siege, Neptune, in a conversation with Apollo before the walls of Troy, spoke of their labors in the service of the Trojan king:

"Hast thou forgot, how, at the monarch's prayer,
We shared the lengthen'd labors of a year?
Troy walls I raised (for such were Jove's commands),
And yon proud bulwarks grew beneath my hands:
Thy task it was to feed the bellowing droves
Along fair Ida's vales and pendant groves."

POPE, *Iliad*, Book XXI.

Long before this, however, the two gods had punished Laomedon very severely for breaking his promise. Apollo, after being restored to heaven, sent a plague upon the city of Troy, and Neptune sent up from the sea an enormous serpent which killed many of the people.

A great serpent from the deep,
Lifting his horrible head above their homes,

Devoured the children.

LEWIS MORRIS.

In this terrible calamity the king asked an oracle in what way the anger of the two gods might be appeased. The answer of the oracle was that a Trojan maiden must each year be given to the monster to be devoured. Every year, therefore, a young girl, chosen by lot, was taken down to the seashore and chained to a rock to become the prey of the serpent. And every year the monster came and swallowed up a Trojan maiden, and then went away and troubled the city no more until the following year, when he returned for another victim. At last the lot fell on He-si'o-ne, the daughter of the king. Deep was Laomedon's grief at the thought of the awful fate to which his child was thus doomed.

But help came at an unexpected moment. While, amid the lamentations of her family and friends, preparations were being made to chain Hesione to the rock, the great hero, Her'cu-les, happened to visit Troy. He was on his way home to Greece, after performing in a distant eastern country one of those great exploits which made him famous in ancient story. The hero undertook to destroy the serpent, and thus save the princess, on condition that he should receive as a reward certain wonderful horses which Laomedon just then had in his possession. These horses were given to Laomedon's grandfather, Tros, on a very interesting occasion. Tros had a son named Gan'y-mede, a youth of wonderful beauty, and Jupiter admired Ganymede so much that he had him carried up to heaven to be cupbearer to the gods—to serve the divine nectar at the banquets on Mount Olympus.

> Godlike Ganymede, most beautiful
> Of men; the gods beheld and caught him up
> To heaven, so beautiful was he, to pour

Michael Clarke

The wine to Jove, and ever dwell with them.

BRYANT, *Iliad*, Book XX.

To compensate Tros for the loss of his son, Jupiter gave him four magnificent horses of immortal breed and marvelous fleetness. These were the horses which Hercules asked as his reward for destroying the serpent. As there was no other way of saving the life of his daughter, Laomedon consented. Hercules then went down to the seashore, bearing in his hand the huge club which he usually carried, and wearing his lion-skin over his shoulders. This was the skin of a fierce lion he had strangled to death in a forest in Greece, and he always wore it when going to perform any of his heroic feats.

When Hesione had been bound to the rock, the hero stood beside her and awaited the coming of the serpent. In a short time its hideous form emerged from beneath the waves, and darting forward it was about to seize the princess, when Hercules rushed upon it, and with mighty strokes of his club beat the monster to death. Thus was the king's daughter saved and all Troy delivered from a terrible scourge. But when the hero claimed the reward that had been agreed upon, and which he had so well earned, Laomedon again proved himself to be a man who was neither honest nor grateful. Disregarding his promise, and forgetful, too, of what he and his people had already suffered as a result of his breach of faith with the two gods, he refused to give Hercules the horses.

The hero at once went away from Troy, but not without resolving to return at a convenient time and punish Laomedon. This he did, not long afterwards, when he had completed the celebrated "twelve labors" at which he had been set by a Grecian king, whom Jupiter commanded him to serve for a period of years because of an offense he had committed. One of these labors was the killing of the lion.

Another was the destroying of the Ler'næ-an hydra, a frightful serpent with many heads, which for a long time had been devouring man and beast in the district of Ler'na in Greece.

Having accomplished his twelve great labors and ended his term of service, Hercules collected an army and a fleet, and sailed to the shores of Troas. He then marched against the city, took it by surprise, and slew Laomedon and all his sons, with the exception of Po-dar'ces, afterwards called Priam. This prince had tried to persuade his father to fulfill the engagement with Hercules, for which reason his life was spared. He was made a slave, however, as was done in ancient times with prisoners taken in war. But Hesione ransomed her brother, giving her gold-embroidered veil as the price of his freedom. From this time he was called Priam, a word which in the Greek language means "purchased." Hesione also prevailed upon Hercules to restore Priam to his right as heir to his father's throne, and so he became king of Troy. Hesione herself was carried off to Greece, where she was given in marriage to Tel'a-mon, king of Sal'a-mis, a friend of Hercules.

Priam reigned over his kingdom of Troas many years in peace and prosperity. His wife and queen, the virtuous Hec'u-ba, was a daughter of a Thracian king. They had nineteen children, many of whom became famous during the great siege. Their eldest son, Hec'tor, was the bravest of the Trojan heroes. Their son Par'is it was, as we shall see, who brought upon his country the disastrous war. Another son, Hel'e-nus, and his sister Cas-san'dra, were celebrated soothsayers.

Cassandra was a maiden of remarkable beauty. The god Apollo loved her so much that he offered to grant her any request if she would accept him as her husband. Cassandra consented and asked for the power of foretelling events, but

Michael Clarke

when she received it, she slighted the god and refused to perform her promise. Apollo was enraged at her conduct, yet he could not take back the gift he had bestowed. He decreed, however, that no one should believe or pay any attention to her predictions, true though they should be. And so when Cassandra foretold the evils that were to come upon Troy, even her own people would not credit her words. They spoke of her as the "mad prophetess."

Cassandra cried, and cursed the unhappy hour;
Foretold our fate; but by the god's decree,
All heard, and none believed the prophecy.

VERGIL.

The first sorrow in the lives of King Priam and his good queen came a short time before the birth of Paris, when Hecuba dreamed that her next child would bring ruin upon his family and native city. This caused the deepest distress to Priam and Hecuba, especially when the soothsayer Æs'a-cus declared that the dream would certainly be fulfilled. Then, though they were tender and loving parents, they made up their minds to sacrifice their own feelings rather than that such a calamity should befall their country. When the child was born, the king, therefore, ordered it to be given to Ar-che-la'us, one of the shepherds of Mount Ida, with instructions to expose it in a place where it might be destroyed by wild beasts. The shepherd, though very unwilling to do so cruel a thing, was obliged to obey, but on returning to the spot a few days afterwards he found the infant boy alive and unhurt. Some say that the child had been nursed and carefully tended by a she-bear. Archelaus was so touched with pity at the sight of the innocent babe smiling in his face, that he took the boy to his cottage, and, giving him the name Paris, brought him up as one of his own family.

With the herdsmen on Mount Ida, Paris spent his early years, not knowing that he was King Priam's son. He was a brave youth, and of exceeding beauty.

> "His sunny hair
> Cluster'd about his temples like a god's."

TENNYSON, *Œnone*.

He was skilled, too, in all athletic exercises, he was a bold huntsman, and so brave in defending the shepherds against the attacks of robbers that they called him Alexander, a name which means a protector of men. Thus the young prince became a favorite with the people who lived on the hills. Very happy he was amongst them, and amongst the flocks which his good friend and foster father, Archelaus, gave him to be his own. He was still more happy in the company of the charming nymph Œ-no'ne, the daughter of a river god; and he loved her and made her his wife. But this happiness was destined not to be of long duration. The Fates[A] had decreed it otherwise. Œnone the beautiful, whose sorrows have been the theme of many poets, was to lose the love of the young shepherd prince, and the dream of Hecuba was to have its fulfillment.

> The Fate
> That rules the will of Jove had spun the days
> Of Paris and Œnone.

QUINTUS SMYRNÆUS.

[Footnote A: The Fates were the three sisters, Clo'tho, Lach'e-sis, and At'ro-pos, powerful goddesses who controlled the birth and life of mankind, Clotho, the youngest, presided over the moment of birth, and held a distaff in her hand; Lachesis spun out the thread of human existence (all the events and action's of man's life); and Atropos, with a pair of shears which she always carried, cut this thread at the moment of death.]

II. THE JUDGMENT OF PARIS

It was through a quarrel among the three goddesses, Juno, Venus, and Minerva, that Œnone, the fair nymph of Mount Ida, met her sad fate, and that the destruction of Troy was brought about. The strife arose on the occasion of the marriage of Pe'leus and The'tis. Peleus was a king of Thes'sa-ly, in Greece, and one of the great heroes of those days. Thetis was a daughter of the sea god Ne're-us, who had fifty daughters, all beautiful sea nymphs, called "Ne-re'i-des," from the name of their father. Their duty was to attend upon the greater sea gods, and especially to obey the orders of Neptune.

Thetis was so beautiful that Jupiter himself wished to marry her, but the Fates told him she was destined to have a son who would be greater than his father. The king of heaven having no desire that a son of his should be greater than himself, gave up the idea of wedding the fair nymph of the sea, and consented that she should be the wife of Peleus, who had long loved and wooed her. But Thetis, being a goddess, was unwilling to marry a mortal man. However, she at last consented, and all the gods and goddesses, with one exception, were present at the marriage feast.

> For in the elder time, when truth and worth
> Were still revered and cherished here on earth,
> The tenants of the skies would oft descend

　　　　Michael Clarke

To heroes' spotless homes, as friend to friend;
There meet them face to face, and freely share
In all that stirred the hearts of mortals there.

CATULLUS (Martin's tr.).

The one exception was E'ris, or Dis-cor'di-a, the goddess of discord. This evil-minded deity had at one time been a resident of Olympus, but she caused so much dissension and quarreling there that Jupiter banished her forever from the heavenly mansions. The presence of such a being as a guest on so happy an occasion was not very desirable, and therefore no invitation was sent to her.

Thus slighted, the goddess of discord resolved to have revenge by doing all that she could to disturb the peace and harmony of the marriage feast. With this evil purpose she suddenly appeared in the midst of the company, and threw on the table a beautiful golden apple, on which were inscribed the words, "Let it be given to the fairest."

"This was cast upon the board,
When all the full-faced presence of the gods
Ranged in the halls of Peleus; whereupon
Rose feud, with question unto whom 'twere due."

TENNYSON, *Œnone*.

At once all the goddesses began to claim the glittering prize of beauty. Each contended that she was the "fairest," and therefore should have the

"fruit of pure Hesperian gold
That smelt ambrosially."

But soon the only competitors were Juno, Venus, and Minerva, the other goddesses having withdrawn their claims.

The contest then became more bitter, and at last Jupiter was called upon to act as judge in the dispute. This delicate task the king of heaven declined to undertake. He knew that whatever way he might decide, he would be sure to offend two of the three goddesses, and thereby destroy the peace of his own household. It was necessary, however, that an umpire should be chosen to put an end to the strife, and doubtless it was the decree of the Fates that the lot should fall on the handsome young shepherd of Mount Ida. His wisdom and prudence were well known to the gods, and all seemed to agree that he was a fit person to decide so great a contest.

Paris was therefore appointed umpire. By Jupiter's command the golden apple was sent to him, to be given to that one of the three goddesses whom he should judge to be the most beautiful. The goddesses themselves were directed to appear before him on Mount Ida, so that, beholding their charms, he might be able to give a just decision. The English poet, Tennyson, in his poem "Œnone," gives a fine description of the three contending deities standing in the presence of the Trojan prince, each in her turn trying, by promise of great reward, to persuade him to declare in her favor. Juno spoke first, and she offered to bestow kingly power and immense wealth upon Paris, if he would award the prize to her.

> "She to Paris made
> Proffer of royal power, ample rule
> Unquestion'd. . . . .
> 'Honor,' she said, 'and homage, tax and toll,
> From many an inland town and haven large.'"

Minerva next addressed the judge, and she promised him great wisdom and knowledge, as well as success in war, if he would give the apple to her.

Then Venus approached the young prince, who all the while

held the golden prize in his hand. She had but few words to say, for she was confident in the power of her beauty and the tempting bribe she was about to offer.

> "She with a subtle smile in her mild eyes,
> The herald of her triumph, drawing nigh
> Half-whisper'd in his ear, 'I promise thee
> The fairest and most loving wife in Greece.'
> She spoke and laugh'd."

The subtle smile and the whispered promise won the heart of Paris. Forgetful of Œnone, and disregarding the promises of the other goddesses, he awarded the prize to Venus.

> He consign'd
> To her soft hand the fruit of burnished rind;
> And foam-born Venus grasp'd the graceful meed,
> Of war, of evil war, the quickening seed.

> COLUTHUS (Elton's tr.).

Such was the famous judgment of Paris. It was perhaps a just decision, for it may be supposed that Venus, being the goddess of beauty, was really the most beautiful of the three. But the story does not give us a very high idea of the character of Paris, who now no longer took pleasure in the company of Œnone. All his thoughts and affections were turned away from her by the promise of Venus. He had grown weary, too, of his simple and innocent life among his flocks and herds on the mountain. He therefore wished much for some adventure that would take him away from scenes which had become distasteful to him.

The opportunity soon came. A member of King Priam's family having died, it was announced that the funeral would be celebrated by athletic games, as was the custom in ancient times. Paris resolved to go down to the city and take part in these games. Prizes were to be offered for competition, and one of the prizes was to be the finest bull that could be picked from the herds on Mount Ida. Now it happened that the bull selected belonged to Paris himself, but it could not be taken without his consent. He was willing, however, to give it for the games on condition that he should be permitted to enter the list of competitors.

The condition was agreed to, and so the shepherd prince parted from Œnone and went to the funeral games at Troy. He intended, perhaps, to return sometime, but it was many years before he saw the fair nymph of Mount Ida again,—not until he was about to die of a wound received from one of the Greeks in the Trojan War. Œnone knew what was to happen, for Apollo had conferred upon her the gift of prophecy, and she warned Paris that if he should go away from her he would bring ruin on himself and his country, telling him also that he would seek for her help when it would be too late to save him. These predictions, as we shall see, were fulfilled. Œnone's grief and despair in her loneliness after the departure of Paris are touchingly described in Tennyson's poem:

"O happy Heaven, how canst thou see my face?
O happy earth, how canst thou bear my weight?
O death, death, death, thou ever-floating cloud,
There are enough unhappy on this earth,
Pass by the happy souls, that love to live:
I pray thee, pass before my light of life,
And shadow all my soul, that I may die.
Thou weighest heavy on the heart within,
Weigh heavy on my eyelids: let me die."

At the athletic games in Troy everybody admired the noble appearance of Paris, but nobody knew who he was. In the competitions he won all the first prizes, for Venus had given him godlike strength and swiftness. He defeated even

Michael Clarke

Hector, who was the greatest athlete of Troy. Hector, angry at finding himself and all the highborn young men of the city beaten by an unknown stranger, resolved to put him to death, and Paris would probably have been killed, had he not fled for safety into the temple of Jupiter. Cassandra, who happened to be in the temple at the time, noticed Paris closely, and observing that he bore a strong resemblance to her brothers, she asked him about his birth and age. From his answers she was satisfied that he was her brother, and she at once introduced him to the king. Further inquiries were then made. The old shepherd, Archelaus, to whom Paris had been delivered in his infancy to be exposed on Mount Ida, was still living, and he came and told his story. Then King Priam and Queen Hecuba joyfully embraced and welcomed their son, never thinking of the terrible dream or of the prophecy of Æsacus. Hector, no longer angry or jealous, was glad to see his brother, and proud of his victories in the games. Everybody rejoiced except Cassandra. She knew the evil which was to come to Troy through Paris, but nobody would give credit to what the "mad prophetess" said.

Thus restored to his high position as a prince of the royal house of Troy, Paris now resided in his father's palace, apparently contented and happy. But the promise made to him on Mount Ida, which he carefully concealed from his family, was always in his mind. His thoughts were ever turned toward Greece, where dwelt the fairest woman of those times. This was Helen, wife of Men-e-la'us, king of Spar'ta, celebrated throughout the ancient world for her matchless beauty. Paris had been promised the fairest woman for his wife, and he felt sure that it could be no other than the far-famed Helen. To Greece therefore he resolved to go, as soon as there should be an excuse for undertaking what was then a long and dangerous voyage of many weeks, though in our day it is no more than a few hours' sail.

The occasion was found when King Priam resolved to send

ambassadors to the island of Salamis to demand the restoration of his sister Hesione, whom Hercules had carried off many years before. Her husband, Telamon, was now dead, but his son A'jax still held her as a prisoner at his court. Priam had never forgotten his sister's love for himself, for she it was, as will be remembered, who redeemed him from slavery and placed him on his father's throne. He now determined that she should be brought back to her native country, and Paris earnestly begged permission to take charge of the expedition which was to be sent to Salamis for that purpose. Priam consented, and a fleet worthy to convey the son of the king of Troy and his retinue to Greece was built by Pher'e-clus, a skillful Trojan craftsman, whom the goddess Minerva (Pallas) had instructed in all kinds of workmanship.

> For loved by Pallas, Pallas did impart
> To him the shipwright's and the builder's art.
> Beneath his hand the fleet of Paris rose,
> The fatal cause of all his country's woes.

POPE, *Iliad*, Book V.

Before the departure of the fleet, Cassandra raised her voice of warning, but as usual her words were not heeded, and so Paris set sail. He reached the shores of Greece in safety; but instead of proceeding to Salamis to demand Hesione from King Ajax, he steered his vessels to the coast of Sparta. This he did under the guidance and direction of Venus, who was now about to fulfill the promise by which she had won the golden prize on Mount Ida.

Landing in Sparta, Paris hastened to the court of Menelaus, where he was hospitably received. The king gave banquets in his honor and invited him to prolong his stay in Sparta, and the beautiful Queen Helen joined in her husband's kind attentions to their guest.

Soon after the arrival of Paris, the king of Sparta received an invitation to take part in a hunting expedition in the island of Crete. Having no suspicion of the evil design of Paris, he accepted the invitation. He departed for Crete, leaving to his queen the duty of entertaining the Trojan prince until his return. Then Paris, taking advantage of the absence of Menelaus, induced Helen to desert her husband and her home, and go with him to Troy. He told her of the promise of Venus, and assured her that she would be received with great honor in his father's palace, and protected against the anger of Menelaus.

> From her husband's stranger-sheltering home
> He tempted Helen o'er the ocean foam.

COLUTHUS (Elton's tr.).

Helen having consented, Paris carried her off in his fleet. At the same time he carried away a vast quantity of treasure in gold and other costly things which belonged to King Menelaus. On the voyage homeward the ships were driven by a storm to the shores of the island of Cran'a-e, where Paris and Helen remained for some time. When at last they reached the Trojan capital they were cordially welcomed by King Priam and Queen Hecuba, and in a short time they were married, and the event was celebrated with great rejoicing.

But all the people of Troy did not take part in this rejoicing. Hector, the son of Priam, and others of his wisest counselors, strongly censured the conduct of Paris, and they advised the king to send Helen back to Sparta. But Priam would not listen to their prudent advice, and so she remained in Troy.

The great beauty of Helen has been celebrated by poets in ancient and modern times. Tennyson, in his "Dream of Fair

Women," introduces her as one of the forms of the vision he describes:

> "I saw a lady within call,
> Stiller than chisell'd marble, standing there;
> A daughter of the gods, divinely tall,
> And most divinely fair."

III. THE LEAGUE AGAINST TROY

The carrying off of Helen was the cause of the Trojan War. Menelaus, upon hearing what Paris had done, immediately returned to Sparta, and began to make preparations to avenge the wrong. He called upon the other kings and princes of Greece to join him with their armies and fleets in a war against Troy. They were bound to do this by an oath they had taken at the time of the marriage of Helen and Menelaus.

Helen was the daughter of Tyn'da-rus, who was king of Sparta before Menelaus. Some say that she was the daughter of Jupiter, and that Tyndarus was her stepfather. But from her infancy she was brought up at the royal palace of Sparta as the daughter of Tyndarus and his wife, Le'da. When she became old enough to marry, the fame of her great beauty drew many of the young princes of Greece to Sparta, all competing for her favor, and each hoping to win her for his wife. This placed Tyndarus in a difficulty. He was alarmed at the sight of so many suitors for the hand of his daughter, for he knew that he could not give her to one without offending all the rest. He therefore resolved to adopt the advice of Ulysses, the prince of Ith'a-ca (an island on the west coast of Greece). Ulysses, also named O-dys'seus, was famed for great wisdom as well as valor in war.

> Ulysses, man of many arts,
> Son of Laertes, reared in Ithaca,

That rugged isle, and skilled in every form
Of shrewd device and action wisely planned.

BRYANT, *Iliad*, Book III.

Ulysses had himself been one of the suitors for Helen, but he saw that among so many competitors he had little chance of success. Besides, he had fallen in love with Pe-nel'o-pe, the niece of Tyndarus. He therefore withdrew from the contest, and he offered to suggest a plan for settling the difficulty about Helen, if Tyndarus would give him Penelope to be his wife. Tyndarus consented. Ulysses then advised that Helen should choose for herself which of the princes she would have for her husband, but that before she did so, all the suitors should pledge themselves by oath to submit to her decision, and engage that if any one should take her away from the husband of her choice, they would all join in punishing the offender.

If any dared to seize and bear her off,
All would unite in arms, and lay his town
Level with the ground.

EURIPIDES (Potter's tr.).

The Grecian princes consented to this proposal. They all, including Ulysses himself, took the required oath. Helen then made choice of Menelaus, to whom she was immediately married with great pomp and popular rejoicing. On the death of Tyndarus, Menelaus became king of Sparta, and he and his beautiful queen lived and reigned together in prosperity and happiness until the ill-fated visit of Paris.

Menelaus was the brother of Ag-a-mem'non, king of My-ce'næ, one of the most powerful and wealthy of the kings of Hel'las, as Greece was anciently called. Their father, A'treus, was a son of the hero Pe'lops, who conquered the greater part of the peninsula named from him the Pel-oponne'sus, and who was the grandson of Jupiter. Agamemnon, or A-tri'des (son of Atreus), as he is often called, was commander in chief of all the Greek armies during the siege of Troy. From his high rank and authority Homer calls him the "king of men" and the "king of kings." He is sometimes also called "king of all Ar'gos," a powerful kingdom near Mycenæ, and from this name the Greeks are sometimes called "Ar'gives." The royal scepter which Agamemnon bore in his hands when addressing his soldiers was made by Vulcan for Jupiter.

> The king of kings his awful figure raised;
> High in his hand the golden sceptre blazed;
> The golden sceptre, of celestial flame,
> By Vulcan formed, from Jove to Hermes came:
> To Pelops he the immortal gift resign'd;
> The immortal gift great Pelops left behind.

POPE, *Iliad*, Book II.

The kings and princes of Hellas, who met at the call of Menelaus, decided, after some discussion of the matter, that before declaring war against Troy it would be well to try to obtain satisfaction by peaceful means. They therefore sent ambassadors to Troy to demand the restoration of Helen and the treasures which Paris had carried off. Di'o-mede, king of Æ-to'lia, and the wise Ulysses, were chosen for this mission. Menelaus volunteered to accompany them, thinking that he might be able to persuade his wife to return to her home.

When the Greek ambassadors arrived in the Trojan capital they were respectfully received by the king. During their stay in the city they were entertained at the residence of An-te'nor, one of Priam's ministers of state, who had the wisdom to disapprove of the action of Paris, and to advise that the Spartan queen should be given back to her husband. Antenor much admired the appearance and eloquence of Ulysses, which are thus described in the Iliad:

"But when Ulysses rose, in thought profound,
His modest eyes he fixed upon the ground;
As one unskilled or dumb, he seem'd to stand,
Nor raised his head, nor stretch'd his sceptred hand;
But, when he speaks, what elocution flows!
Soft as the fleeces of descending snows,
The copious accents fall, with easy art;
Melting they fall, and sink into the heart!"

POPE, *Iliad*, Book III.

But the eloquence of Ulysses was of no avail. King Priam, blinded by his love for his son, saw not the threatened danger, and he refused the demand of the ambassadors. Menelaus was not even permitted to see his wife. Ulysses and his companions then returned to Greece, and at once preparations for war with Troy were commenced.

These preparations occupied a very long time. Ten years were spent in getting together the vast force, which in more than a thousand ships was carried across the Ægean Sea to the Trojan shores, from the port of Au'lis on the east coast-of Greece. Some of the Hel-len'ic (Greek) princes were very unwilling to join the expedition, as they knew that the struggle would be a tedious and perilous one. Even Ulysses, who, as we have seen, had first proposed the suitors' oath at Sparta, was at the last moment unwilling to go. He had now become king of Ithaca, his father, La-er'tes, having retired from the cares of government, and he would gladly have remained in his happy island home with his young wife, Penelope, and his infant son, Te-lem'a-chus, both of whom he tenderly loved.

But the man of many arts could not be spared from the Trojan War. He paid no heed, however, to the messages sent to him asking him to join the army at Aulis. Agamemnon resolved, therefore, to go himself to Ithaca to persuade Ulysses to take part in the expedition. He was accompanied by his brother Menelaus, and by a chief named Pal-a-me'des, a very wise and learned man as well as a brave warrior. As soon as Ulysses heard of their arrival in Ithaca, he pretended to be insane, and he tried by a very amusing stratagem to make them believe that he was really mad. Dressing himself in his best clothes, and going down to the seashore, he began to plow the beach with a horse and an *ox* yoked together, and to scatter salt upon the sand instead of seed.

Palamedes, however, was more than a match in artifice for the Ithacan king. Taking Telemachus from the arms of his nurse, he placed the infant on the sand in front of the plowing team. Ulysses quickly turned the animals aside to avoid injuring his child, thus proving that he was not mad but in full possession of his senses. The king of Ithaca was therefore obliged to join the expedition to Troy. With twelve ships well manned he sailed from his rugged island, which he did not again see for twenty years. Ten years he spent at the siege, and ten on his homeward voyage, during which he met with the wonderful adventures that Homer describes in the Odyssey.

Ulysses had his revenge upon Palamedes in a manner very unworthy of a brave man. In the camp before Troy, during the siege, he bribed one of the servants of Palamedes to conceal a sum of money in his master's tent. He then forged a letter, which he read before a council of the Greek generals, saying that Palamedes had taken it from a Trojan prisoner. This letter was written as if by King Priam to Palamedes, thanking him for the information he had given regarding the plans of the Greeks, and mentioning money as having been sent him in reward for his services. The Greek generals at once ordered a search to be made in the tent of Palamedes, and the money being found where it had been hidden by direction of Ulysses, the unfortunate Palamedes was immediately put to death as a traitor.

> Palamedes, not unknown to fame,
> Who suffered from the malice of the times,
> Accused and sentenced for pretended crimes.

VERGIL.

It is said that Palamedes was the inventor of weights and measures, and of the games of chess and backgammon, and that it was he who first placed sentinels round a camp and gave them a watchword.

There was another of the Greek princes whose help in the Trojan War was obtained only by an ingenious trick. This was the famous A-chil'les. He was the son of Peleus and Thetis, at whose marriage feast Eris threw the apple of discord on the table. The prophecy that Thetis would have a son greater than his father was fulfilled in Achilles, the bravest of the Greeks at the Trojan War, and the principal hero of Homer's Iliad.

Thetis educated her son with great care. She had him instructed in all the accomplishments fitting for princes of those times. When he was an infant she dipped him in the river Styx, which, it was believed, made it impossible for any weapon wielded by mortal hands to wound him. But the water did not touch the child's heel by which his mother held him when she plunged him in the river, and it was in this part that he received the wound of which he died.

Notwithstanding his being dipped in the Styx, Thetis was afraid to let Achilles go to the Trojan War, for Jupiter had told her that he would be killed if he took part in it. For this reason, as soon as she heard that the Grecian princes were gathering their forces, she secretly sent the youth to the court of Lyc-o-me'des, king of the island of Scy'ros. Here Achilles, dressed like a young girl, resided as a companion of the king's daughters. But Cal'chas, the soothsayer of the Grecian army, told the chiefs that without the help of Achilles Troy could not be taken.

Calchas the wise, the Grecian priest and guide,
That sacred seer, whose comprehensive view,
The past, the present, and the future knew.

POPE, *Iliad*, Book I.

Calchas, however, could not tell where Achilles was to be found, and when they applied to Peleus, he too was unable or unwilling to tell them. In this difficulty the wily king of Ithaca did good service. After much inquiry he discovered that Achilles was at Scyros with the king's daughters. He soon made his way to the island, but here there was a new difficulty. He had never seen the young prince, and how was he to know him? But he devised a scheme which proved entirely successful. Equipping himself as a peddler, he went to the royal palace, exhibiting jewelry and other fancy articles to attract the attention of the ladies of the family. He also had some beautiful weapons of war among his wares.

As soon as he appeared, the maidens gathered about him and began examining the jewels. But one of the group eagerly seized a weapon, and handled it with much skill and pleasure. Satisfied that this was the young prince of whom he was in search, the pretended peddler announced his name and told why he had come. Achilles, for it was he, gladly agreed to take part with his countrymen in their great expedition, and he immediately returned to Phthi'a, the capital of his father's kingdom of Thessaly. There he lost no time in making all necessary preparations. Soon afterwards he sailed for Aulis with the brave Myr'mi-dons, as his soldiers were called, accompanied also by his devoted friend and constant companion, Pa-tro'clus.

> Full fifty ships beneath Achilles' care,
> The Achaians, Myrmidons, Hellenians bear;
> Thessalians all, though various in their name;
> The same their nation, and their chief the same.

> POPE, *Iliad*, Book II.

Agamemnon, the commander in chief of the great host, sailed with a hundred ships from his kingdom of Mycenæ, and his brother Menelaus, eager for vengeance upon the Trojans, sailed with sixty ships and a strong force of brave Spartans.

> Great Agamemnon rules the numerous band,
> A hundred vessels in long order stand,
> And crowded nations wait his dread command.
> High on the deck the king of men appears,
> And his refulgent arms in triumph wears;
> Proud of his host, unrivall'd in his reign,
> In silent pomp he moves along the main.
> His brother follows, and to vengeance warms,
> The hardy Spartans, exercised in arms: . . . . . .
> These, o'er the bending ocean, Helen's cause,
> In sixty ships with Menelaus draws.

> POPE, *Iliad* Book II.

Among the other great warriors of Hellas who joined the expedition was Nes'tor, the venerable king of Py'los, distinguished for his eloquence, wisdom, and prudence.

> In ninety sail, from Pylos' sandy coast,
> Nestor the sage conducts his chosen host.

> POPE, *Iliad*, Book II.

The ancients believed that Nestor outlived three generations of men, which some suppose to have been three hundred years. From this it was a custom of the ancient Greeks and Romans, when wishing a long and happy life to their friends, to wish them to live as long as Nestor.

> Experienced Nestor, in persuasion skill'd;
> Words, sweet as honey, from his lips distill'd;
> Two generations now had pass'd away,
> Wise by his rules, and happy by his sway;
> Two ages o'er his native realm he reign'd,
> And now the example of the third remain'd.

POPE, *Iliad,* Book I.

The two Ajaxes were also renowned warriors of the Grecian army,—Ajax Telamon and Ajax O-i'leus, so called from the names of their fathers. Telamon was the king of Salamis, to whom, as has been told, Hercules gave Laomedon's daughter, Hesione. His son Ajax, a man of huge stature and giant strength, was, next to Achilles, the bravest of all the Greeks who went to the Trojan War.

> With these appear the Salaminian bands,
> Whom the gigantic Telamon commands;
> In twelve black ships to Troy they steer their course,
> And with the great Athenians join their force.

POPE, *Iliad*, Book II.

Ajax Oileus, king of Lo'cris, was less in stature than his namesake, but few excelled him in the use of the spear or in swiftness of foot. He commanded forty ships in the great expedition.

> Fierce Ajax led the Locrian squadrons on,
> Ajax the less, Oileus' valiant son;

Skill'd to direct the flying dart aright;
Swift in pursuit, and active in the fight.

POPE, *Iliad*, Book II

Two other valiant warriors, who led eighty ships each to the great muster, were Diomede, king of Argos, and I-dom'e-neus, king of Crete,—the "spear-renowned Idomeneus."

Crete's hundred cities pour forth all her sons.
These march'd, Idomeneus, beneath thy care.

POPE, *Iliad*, Book II.

When at length all the kings and princes were assembled at Aulis, the vast fleet numbered 1185 ships, according to the account given by Homer. The total number of men which the ships carried is not known, but it is probable that it was not less than 100,000, as the largest of the vessels contained about 120, and the smallest 50 men each.

Such was the mighty host that Hellas marshaled to punish Troy for the crime committed by Paris. Before setting out on so important an expedition the Greek chiefs deemed it proper, according to the custom of the ancients, to offer sacrifices to the gods, that their undertaking might have the favor of heaven. Altars were therefore erected, and the sacred services were carried out in due order. On these occasions animals—very frequently oxen—were killed, and portions of their flesh consumed by fire, such sacrifices being supposed to be very pleasing to the gods.

While the Grecian chiefs were engaged in their religious ceremonies, the greater part of the army having already gone aboard the ships, they were startled at beholding a serpent dart out from beneath one of the altars, and, gliding along the ground, ascend a plane tree which grew close by. At the top of the tree was a nest containing eight young birds. The serpent devoured them, and immediately afterwards seized and devoured the mother bird, which had been fluttering around the nest. Then suddenly, before the eyes of the astonished Greeks, the reptile turned into stone. Amazed at this occurrence, and believing it to have some connection with their expedition, the assembled chiefs asked the soothsayer Calchas to explain what it meant. The seer replied, telling them that it was a sign that the war upon which they were about to enter would last ten years.

"For us, indeed," said he, "Jupiter has shown a great sign. As this serpent has devoured the young of the sparrow, eight in number, and herself, the mother of the brood, was the ninth, so must we for as many years wage war, but in the tenth year we shall take the city."

This story was eloquently told by Ulysses in the Greek camp before Troy, when in the tenth year of the siege, many of the troops, having grown weary of the war, desired to return to their homes.

IV. BEGINNING OF THE WAR

The Greek chiefs, nothing daunted by the words of Calchas, now set sail with their immense fleet. Though the war was to be a long one, they were encouraged by the prophecy that they were to be the conquerors.

Their first experience was not very fortunate. They safely crossed the Ægean Sea, but instead of steering for Troy, the pilots, through either ignorance or mistake, brought the vessels to the shore on the coast of Teu-thra'ni-a, a district in the kingdom of Mys'i-a, lying southeast of Troas. Here the Greeks landed, but they were at once attacked by Tel'e-phus, the king of that country, who came down upon them with a strong force, and drove them back to their ships after a battle in which many of them were killed. They would probably have fared much worse had it not been for the friendly aid of Bac'chus, the god of wine. While Telephus was fighting at the head of his men he tripped and fell over a vine, which the god had caused to spring up suddenly from the earth at his feet. As he lay flat on the ground Achilles rushed forward and severely wounded him with a thrust of his spear.

The Greeks, however, were obliged to take to the sea, and soon afterward a great storm arose, which destroyed many of their vessels. Owing to this misfortune they had to return to Aulis, where they set about repairing their damaged ships and getting ready to start again. While the Greeks were thus engaged, they were surprised by the appearance of King Telephus, who came to their camp to beg Achilles to cure his wound, an oracle he had consulted having told him that he could be cured only by the person who had wounded him.

Achilles was at first unwilling to comply with the request of Telephus, but Ulysses advised him to do so. Telephus was one of the sons of Hercules, and it had been decreed that without the help of a son of that hero Troy could not be taken. Moreover, he was a son-in-law of Priam, and his country lay close to where the war was to be carried on. For these reasons Ulysses wished to make him friendly to the Greeks, and so he persuaded Achilles to cure the Teuthranian king. Achilles did this by dropping into the wound portions of the rust from the point of his spear. Telephus was so grateful that he joined the expedition against Troy, and undertook to pilot the Grecian fleet to the Trojan coast.

But another difficulty now stood in the way of the Greeks. Their fleet was once more ready for departure, but the winds were unfavorable. In ancient times they could not make a sea voyage when the winds were against them. Their ships were very small, and were moved only by oars and sails. Homer gives us a good idea of the ancient system of navigation, where he tells, in the Odyssey, about young Telemachus setting out on a voyage in search of his father, Ulysses:

Telemachus went up
The vessel's side, but Pallas first embarked,
And at the stern sat down, while next to her
Telemachus was seated. Then the crew
Cast loose the fastenings and went all on board,
And took their places on the rowers' seats,
While blue-eyed Pallas sent a favoring breeze,
A fresh wind from the west, that murmuring swept
The dark-blue main. Telemachus gave forth
The word to wield the tackle; they obeyed,

And raised the fir-tree mast, and, fitting it
Into its socket, bound it fast with cords,
And drew and spread with firmly twisted ropes
The shining sails on high. The steady wind
Swelled out the canvas in the midst; the ship
Moved on, the dark sea roaring round her keel,
As swiftly through the waves she cleft her way.

BRYANT, *Odyssey*, Book II.

For many days the Greek chiefs at Aulis waited for favoring breezes, but none came.

"The troops
Collected and embodied, here we sit
Inactive, and from Aulis wish to sail   In vain."

EURIPIDES (Potter's tr.).

At last the soothsayer Calchas told them that the easterly winds which prevented them from sailing were caused by the anger of Di-an'a. Diana was the goddess of hunting, and there was one of her sacred groves in the neighborhood of Aulis. In this grove King Agamemnon went hunting during the time the ships were being repaired after the storm, and he killed one of Diana's favorite deer. He even boasted that he was a greater hunter than Diana herself. This enraged the goddess, and Calchas said that her anger could be appeased only by the offering up of Agamemnon's daughter, Iph-i-ge-ni'a, as a sacrifice.

The feelings of the father may be easily imagined. He heard the announcement of the soothsayer with the utmost horror, and he declared that he would withdraw from the expedition rather than permit his child to be put to death. But Ulysses and the other princes begged him to remember that the honor of their country was at stake. They said that if he should withdraw, the great cause for which they had labored for ten years would be lost, and the Trojan insult to his own family and to all Greece would remain unpunished.

At last Agamemnon consented, and messengers were sent to Mycenæ to bring Iphigenia to Aulis. The king was even persuaded to deceive his wife, Clyt-em-nes'tra. Knowing that she would not allow her daughter to be taken away for such a purpose, he wrote a letter to the queen, saying that Iphigenia had been chosen to be the wife of Achilles, and that he wished the marriage ceremony to be performed before the departure of the young prince for Troy.

> "I wrote, I seal'd
> A letter to my wife, that she should send
> Her daughter to Achilles as a bride   Affianc'd."

> EURIPIDES (Potter's tr.).

Clytemnestra agreed to the proposal, happy at the thought of her daughter being married to so great a prince as Achilles. Iphigenia accordingly accompanied the messengers to the Greek camp at Aulis. When she learned of the terrible fate to which she had been doomed, she threw herself at her father's feet and piteously implored his protection. But her tears and entreaties were in vain. The agonized father had now no power to save her, for the whole army demanded that the will of the goddess should be obeyed. Preparations for the awful sacrifice were therefore made, and when everything was ready, the beautiful young princess was led to the altar. Tennyson, in his "Dream of Fair Women," has these lines about Iphigenia at Aulis:

> "I was cut off from hope in that sad place,
> Which men called Aulis in those iron years:
> My father held his hand upon his face;
> I, blinded with my tears,

Still strove to speak: my voice was thick with sighs
As in a dream. Dimly I could descry
The stern, black-bearded kings with wolfish eyes,
Waiting to see me die."

But Iphigenia was not sacrificed after all. Her innocence excited the pity even of Diana, and at the last moment the goddess snatched the weeping maiden away in a cloud, and left in her place a beautiful deer to be offered up as a sacrifice. She carried the princess off to Tau'ri-ca, a country bordering the Black Sea, and there Iphigenia remained for many years, serving as a priestess in Diana's temple.

The anger of Diana being appeased, favorable winds now began to blow, and the Greeks again set sail. This time they had a more fortunate voyage. Piloted by Telephus, the fleet crossed the Ægean Sea, and safely reached the coast of Troas. But here Calchas made another discouraging prophecy. He declared that the first Greek who stepped on Trojan soil would be killed in the first fight with the enemy. This the oracle at Delphi had also foretold. There was some hesitation, therefore, about landing, for the army of King Priam was ranged along the beach prepared for battle with the invaders.

This was the occasion of an heroic act by Pro-tes-i-la'us, king of Phyl'a-ce in Thessaly, who boldly leaped ashore as soon as the vessels touched the land. The prediction of Calchas was soon fulfilled. Protesilaus was struck dead in the first fight by a spear launched by the hands of the Trojan leader, Hector. The bravery of the Thessalian king, and the grief of his queen, La-od-a-mi'a, when she heard of his death, have been much celebrated in song and story.

Protesilaus the brave,
Who now lay silent in the gloomy grave:
The first who boldly touch'd the Trojan shore,

And dyed a Phrygian lance with Grecian gore;
There lies, far distant from his native plain;
And his sad consort beats her breast in vain.

POPE, *Iliad*, Book II.

Laodamia in her sorrow prayed to the gods that she might see her husband again on earth. Jupiter heard her prayer, and he ordered Mercury to conduct Protesilaus from Hades, the land of the dead, to Thessaly, to remain with Laodamia for the space of three hours.

Laodamia was happy for the brief time allowed her to enjoy again the companionship of her beloved Protesilaus, and she listened with pride to the story of his brave deed on the Trojan shore.

"Thou know'st, the Delphic oracle foretold
That the first Greek who touched the Trojan strand
Should die; but me the threat could not withhold:
A generous cause a victim did demand;
And forth I leapt upon the sanely plain;
A self-devoted chief—by Hector slain."

WORDSWORTH, *Laodamia*.

But the happy moments flew swiftly by, and when the three hours had passed, Mercury returned to take the hero back to the world of shades. The parting was too much for the fond Laodamia. She died of grief as her husband disappeared from her sight.

Protesilaus was buried on the Trojan shore, and around his grave, it is said, there grew very wonderful trees. These trees withered away as soon as their tops reached high enough to be seen from the city of Troy. Then fresh trees sprang up from their roots, and withered in like manner when they reached the same height, and so this marvelous growth and decay continued for ages.

> Upon the side
> Of Hellespont (such faith was entertained)
> A knot of spiry trees for ages grew
> From out the tomb of him for whom she died;
> And ever, when such stature they had gained
> That Ilium's walls were subject to their view,
> The trees' tall summits withered at the sight;
> A constant interchange of growth and blight!

WORDSWORTH, *Laodamia.*

The heroic act of Protesilaus was the beginning of the great war. Before he fell himself he slew many of the enemy, and hosts of his countrymen, encouraged by his example, poured from their ships and encountered the Trojans in fierce conflict. In this first battle the Greeks were victorious. Though Hector and his brave troops fought valiantly they were driven back from the shore, and compelled to take refuge within the strong walls of the city.

The Trojans were well prepared for the war. King Priam had not been idle while the Greek leaders were mustering their forces. From all parts of his kingdom he had gathered immense supplies of provisions, and the princes and chiefs of Troas came with large armies to defend their king and country. The most celebrated of these chiefs was the hero Æ-ne'as, son of An-chi'ses and the goddess Venus. He comman-ded the Dardanian forces, and had as his lieutenants the two brave warriors, Ac'a-mas and Ar-chil'o-chus.

> Divine Æneas brings the Dardan race.
> Archilochus and Acamas divide
> The warrior's toils, and combat by his side.

Michael Clarke

POPE, *Iliad*, Book II.

The Trojans had numerous and powerful allies. Troops were sent to them from the neighboring countries of Phrygia, Mysia, Lyc'i-a and Ca'ri-a. The Lycian forces were led by Sar-pe'don, a son of Jupiter, and a renowned warrior.

> A chief, who led to Troy's beleaguer'd wall
> A host of heroes, and outshined them all.

POPE, *Iliad*, Book XVI.

But the greatest of the heroes who defended Troy, and, with the exception of Achilles, the greatest and bravest of all who took part in the Trojan War, was the famous Hector.

> The boast of nations, the defense of Troy!
> To whom her safety and her fame she owed;
> Her chief, her hero, and almost her god!

POPE, *Iliad*, Book XXII.

So long as Hector lived Troy was safe. When he died, his great rival, Achilles, by whose hand he was slain, rejoiced with the Greeks as if Troy had already fallen.

> "Ye sons of Greece, in triumph bring
> The corpse of Hector, and your pæans sing.
> Be this the song, slow-moving toward the shore,
> 'Hector is dead, and Ilion is no more.'"

POPE, *Iliad*, Book XXII.

But though led by the great Hector, the Trojans, after their first defeat, were unable to keep up the fight in the open field against the vast numbers of the Greeks. Seeing, therefore, that they must depend for safety on the strong walls which

Neptune had built, they drew all their forces into the city, leaving the enemy in possession of the surrounding country.

Then the famous siege of ten years began. The Greeks hauled their ships out of the water, and fixed them on the beach in an upright position supported by props. Close to the vessels, on the land side, they erected their tents, which extended in a long line, one wing, or end, of which was guarded by Achilles, and the other by Ajax Telamon. Between this encampment and the walls of Troy—a distance of three or four miles—many a fierce conflict took place, and many a brave warrior fell during the great contest. For the Trojans, headed by Hector or some other of their chiefs, often came out from the city through the principal gate, called the Scæ'an Gate, which faced the Grecian camp, and fought the enemy in the open plain, on the bank of the celebrated river Simois.

> And from the walls of strong-besieged Troy,
> When their brave hope, bold Hector, march'd to field,
> Stood many Trojan mothers, sharing joy
> To see their youthful son's bright weapons wield;
> And to their hope they such odd action yield,
> That through their light joy seemed to appear,
> Like bright things stain'd, a kind of heavy fear.
>
> And from the strond of Dardan, where they fought,
> To Simois' reedy banks the red blood ran,
> Whose waves to imitate the battle sought
> With swelling ridges; and their ranks began
> To break upon the galled shore, and then
> Retire again, till, meeting greater ranks,
> They join and shoot their foam at Simois' banks.

SHAKESPEARE, *Lucrece*.

Michael Clarke

V. THE WRATH OF ACHILLES

For over nine years the siege was carried on without one side or the other gaining any important victory. The Trojans were protected by their walls, which the Greeks were unable to break down, for the ancients had no such powerful engines of war as those used in armies of the present day. The strongest buildings may now be easily destroyed by cannon; but in those days they had no cannon or gunpowder or dynamite. Success in war in ancient times depended almost entirely on the bravery of the soldiers or on strategy and artifice, in which, as we shall see, the king of Ithaca was much skilled.

The Greek and Trojan warriors fought with swords, axes, bows and arrows, and javelins, or long spears tipped with sharp iron points. Sometimes they used huge stones which the heroes hurled at the foe with the full strength of their powerful arms. They had shields of circular or oval shape, which they wore on the arm to ward off blows, and which could be moved at pleasure so as to cover almost any part of the body. Their chests were protected by corselets or breastplates made of metal, and metal greaves, or boots, incased their legs from the knees to the feet. On their heads they wore helmets, usually of brass.

The chiefs fought in chariots, from which they darted their spears at the enemy with such force and so true an aim as to wound or kill at a considerable distance. The chariots were two-wheeled, open at the back, and often drawn by three horses. They usually carried two warriors, both standing, and the charioteer, or driver, was generally the companion or friend, and not the servant, of the fighters who stood behind him. Sometimes the warriors came down from their chariots and fought hand to hand at close quarters with the enemy. The common soldiers always fought on foot. There were no horse soldiers.

But in the Trojan War success or defeat did not always depend on the bravery of the soldiers or on the skill or strategy of the generals. Very much depended on the gods. We have seen how those divine beings had to do with the events that led to the war. We shall also see them taking part in the battles, sometimes giving victory to one side and sometimes to the other. The Trojan War was in fact as much a war of the gods as of men, and in Homer's story we find Jupiter and Juno and Apollo and Neptune and Venus and Minerva mentioned almost as frequently as the Greek and Trojan heroes. In the beginning of the Iliad we find Apollo sending a plague among the Greeks because of an insult offered to his priest, Chry'ses; for the daughter of Chryses, a beautiful maiden named Chry-se'is, was carried off by Achilles after the taking of The'be, a town of Mysia.

During the long siege the Grecian chiefs extended the war into the surrounding districts. While part of their forces was left at the camp to protect the ships and keep the Trojans cooped up within their walls, expeditions were sent out against many of the towns of Troas, or of the neighboring countries which were allies and supporters of Troy. When the Greeks captured a town they carried off not only the provisions and riches it contained, but also many of its inhabitants, whom they sold as slaves, according to the custom of the time, or kept as slaves in their own service. In one of these expeditions Priam's youngest son, Tro'i-lus, the hero of Shakespeare's play of "Troilus and Cres'si-da," was slain by Achilles.

It was in the tenth year of the war that Thebe was taken, and the maiden Chryseis was captured. About the same time the town of Lyr-nes'sus was seized by an expedition, also led by Achilles, and among the prisoners was a beautiful woman named Bri-se'is. In the division of the spoils among the chiefs, Chryseis fell to the share of Agamemnon, and the maiden Briseis was given to Achilles, who took her to his tent with the intention of making her his wife. But the priest Chryses was deeply grieved at the taking away of his daughter, and he came to the Grecian camp to beg the chiefs to restore her to him. In his hand he bore a golden scepter bound with fillets, or green branches, the emblems of his priestly office, and he also carried with him valuable gifts for King Agamemnon. Being admitted to the presence of the warrior chiefs assembled in council, he begged them to release his child.

> He sued to all, but chief implored for grace
> The brother-kings, of Atreus' royal race.
> "Ye kings and warriors! may your vows be crown'd,
> And Troy's proud walls lie level with the ground.
> May Jove restore you when your toils are o'er
> Safe to the pleasures of your native shore.
> But, oh! relieve a wretched parent's pain,
> And give Chryseis to these arms again."

POPE, *Iliad*, Book I.

Hearing the prayer of the venerable priest, many of the chiefs were moved to pity, and they advised that his request should be granted, but Agamemnon angrily refused.

> He dismissed
> The priest with scorn, and added threatening words:—

"Old man, let me not find thee loitering here,
Beside the roomy ships, or coming back
Hereafter, lest the fillet thou dost bear
And scepter of thy god protect thee not.
This maiden I release not till old age
Shall overtake her in my Argive home,
Far from her native country."

BRYANT, *Iliad*, Book I.

Chryses then departed from the Grecian camp, and as he
returned home in sorrow, walking along the shores of the
sea, he prayed to Apollo to punish the insult thus offered to
his priest.

"O Smintheus! if I ever helped to deck
Thy glorious temple, if I ever burned
Upon thy altar the fat thighs of goats
And bullocks, grant my prayer, and let thy shafts
Avenge upon the Greeks the tears I shed."

BRYANT, *Iliad*, Book I.

Apollo heard the prayer of Chryses, and he sent a deadly
plague upon the Grecian army. With his silver bow, every
clang of which was heard throughout the camp, the archer
god darted his terrible arrows among the Greeks, smiting
them down in great numbers.

He came as comes the night,
And, seated from the ships aloof, sent forth
An arrow; terrible was heard the clang
Of that resplendent bow. At first he smote
The mules and the swift dogs, and then on man
He turned the deadly arrow. All around
Glared evermore the frequent funeral piles.

Michael Clarke

BRYANT, *Iliad*, Book I.

For nine days the arrows of death were sent upon the Greek army, and the funeral piles of the victims were continually burning, for it was the custom in those times to burn the bodies of the dead. On the tenth day of the plague Achilles called a council of the chiefs to consider how the anger of the god might be appeased, and he spoke before them, saying:

"Let us consult some prophet or priest who will tell us why Phœbus Apollo is so much enraged with us, and whether he may, when we shall have offered sacrifices upon his altar, take away this pestilence which is destroying our people."

Then Calchas, the soothsayer, arose and said:

"O Achilles, I can tell why the god is wroth against us, and willing I am to tell it, but perhaps I may irritate the king who rules over all the Argives, and in his anger he may do evil to me. Promise me, therefore, your protection, and I will declare why this plague has come upon the Greeks."

"Fear nothing, O Calchas," answered Achilles. "While I am alive not one of all the Greeks, not even Agamemnon himself, shall harm you."

"Fear nothing, but speak boldly out whate'er
Thou knowest, and declare the will of heaven.
For by Apollo, dear to Jove, whom thou,
Calchas, dost pray to, when thou givest forth
The sacred oracles to men of Greece,
No man, while yet I live, and see the light
Of day, shall lay a violent hand on thee."

BRYANT, *Iliad*, Book I.

Thus encouraged, Calchas announced to the chiefs that Apollo was angry because his priest had been dishonored and insulted by Agamemnon. This was why the people were perishing, and the wrath of the god could be appeased only by restoring Chryseis to her father, and sending a hundred victims to be offered in sacrifice to the god. Upon hearing these words Agamemnon was filled with anger against Calchas.

"Prophet of evil," he exclaimed, "never have you spoken anything good for me. And now you say I must give up the maiden. I shall do so, since I wish not the destruction of the people, but another I must have, for it is not fitting that I alone of all the Argives shall be without a prize."

To this Achilles answered that there was no prize just then that Agamemnon could have. "How can we give you a prize," said he, "since all the spoils have already been divided? We cannot ask the people to return what has been given to them. Be satisfied then to let the maiden go. When we have taken the strong city of Troy we will compensate you fourfold."

"Not so," replied Agamemnon. "If the Greeks give me a suitable prize, I shall be content, but if not, I will seize yours or that of Ajax or Ulysses. This matter, however, we will attend to afterwards. For the present let the maid be sent back to her father, that the wrath of the Far-darter may be appeased."

At this Achilles was very angry, and he said:

"Impudent and greedy man, how can the Greeks fight bravely under your command? As for me, I did not come here to make war against the Trojans because of any quarrel of my own. The Trojans have done no wrong to me. It is to get satisfaction for your brother we have come here in our ships, and we do most of the fighting while to you is given most of the spoils. But now I will return home to Phthia. Perhaps you will then have little treasure to share."

Greatly enraged at this speech, Agamemnon replied in wrathful words: "Go home, by all means, with your ships and your Myrmidons. Other chiefs there are here who will honor me, and I care not for your anger."

"Thus, in turn,
I threaten thee; since Phœbus takes away
Chryseis, I will send her in my ship
And with my friends, and, coming to thy tent,
Will bear away the fair-cheeked maid, thy prize,
Briseis, that thou learn how far I stand
Above thee, and that other chiefs may fear
To measure strength with me, and brave my power."

BRYANT, *Iliad*, Book I.

Furious at this threat, Achilles put his hand to his sword with the intention of slaying Agamemnon, and he had half drawn the weapon from its scabbard, but just at that moment the goddess Minerva stood behind him and caught him by his yellow hair. She had been sent down from heaven by Juno to pacify the hero, for Juno and Minerva were friendly to the Greeks. Ever since the judgment on Mount Ida they hated Paris, and the city and country to which he belonged, and therefore they wished that there should be no strife amongst the Greek chiefs, which would prevent them from taking and destroying the hated city.

Achilles was astonished when he beheld the goddess, who appeared to him alone, being invisible to all the rest. He instantly knew who she was, and he said to her: "O goddess, have you come to witness the insolence of the son of Atreus?

You shall also witness the punishment I shall inflict upon him for his haughtiness."

But Minerva spoke soothing words to the hero:

> "I came from heaven to pacify thy wrath,
> If thou wilt heed my counsel. I am sent
> By Juno the white-armed, to whom ye both
> Are dear, who ever watches o'er you both.
> Refrain from violence; let not thy hand
> Unsheath the sword, but utter with thy tongue
> Reproaches, as occasion may arise,
> For I declare what time shall bring to pass;
> Threefold amends shall yet be offered thee,
> In gifts of princely cost, for this day's wrong.
> Now calm thy angry spirit, and obey."

> BRYANT, *Iliad*, Book I.

Thus Minerva spoke, and Achilles, answering her, said: "Willingly, O goddess, shall I observe your command, though in my soul much enraged, for so it is better, since the gods are ever favorable to those who obey them."

So speaking he put his sword back into its scabbard, while the goddess swiftly returned to Olympus. Then the hero again addressed Agamemnon in bitter words, and he took a solemn oath on the scepter he held in his hand, that he would refuse to help the Greeks when they next should seek his aid for battle with the Trojans.

> "Tremendous oath! inviolate to kings;
> By this I swear:—when bleeding Greece again
> Shall call Achilles, she shall call in vain."

> POPE, *Iliad*, Book I.

Michael Clarke

The venerable Nestor then arose to speak, and he begged the two chiefs to cease quarreling with each other, for the Trojans, he said, would greatly rejoice to hear of strife between the bravest men of the Greeks. He advised Achilles, though of a goddess-mother born, not to contend against his superior in authority, and he entreated Agamemnon not to dishonor Achilles, the bulwark of the Greeks, by taking away the prize which had been allotted to him.

"Forbid it, gods! Achilles should be lost,
The pride of Greece, and bulwark of our host."

POPE, *Iliad*, Book I.

But the wise Nestor advised and entreated in vain. Agamemnon would not yield from his purpose of taking away the prize of Achilles, and so the council of the chiefs came to an end.

Rising from that strife of words, the twain
Dissolved the assembly at the Grecian fleet.

BRYANT, *Iliad*, Book I.

Immediately afterwards, by order of the king, the maiden Chryseis was conducted to her father's home, and sacrifices were offered to Apollo. The anger of the god being thus appeased, the army was relieved from the plague. Then Agamemnon proceeded to carry out his threat against Achilles. Calling two of his officers, or heralds, Tal-thyb'i-us and Eu-ryb'a-tes, he commanded them thus:

"Go ye to where Achilles holds his tent,
And take the fair Briseis by the hand,
And bring her hither. If he yield her not,
I shall come forth to claim her with a band
Of warriors, and it shall be worse for him."

BRYANT, *Iliad*, Book I.

Achilles received the heralds respectfully. He had no blame for them, since they were but messengers. Nor did he refuse to obey the command of the king. He delivered Briseis to the heralds, and they conducted her to the tent of Agamemnon. Thus was committed the deed which brought countless woes upon the Greeks, for Achilles, in deep grief and anger, vowed that he would no more lead his Myrmidons to battle for a king who had so dishonored and insulted him.

"Let these heralds," said he, "be the witnesses before gods and men of the insult offered to me by this tyrant king, and when there shall be need of me again to save the Greeks from destruction, appeal to me shall be in vain."

Such was the origin of the wrath of Achilles, which is the subject of Homer's Iliad. The Iliad is not a complete story of the Trojan War, but an account of the disasters which happened to the Greeks through the anger of Achilles. The poem, indeed, relates the events of only fifty-eight days, but they were events of the highest interest and they were very numerous. It is remarked by Pope that the subject of the Iliad is the shortest and most single ever chosen by any poet. Yet Homer has supplied a vaster variety of incidents, a greater number of councils, speeches, battles, and events of all kinds, than are to be found in any other poem.

The Iliad begins with the wrath of Achilles, which in the first line of the first book is announced as the poet's theme:

Achilles' wrath, to Greece the direful spring
Of woes unnumber'd, heavenly goddess, sing!
That wrath which hurl'd to Pluto's gloomy reign
The souls of mighty chiefs untimely slain;
Whose limbs unburied on the naked shore,
Devouring dogs and hungry vultures tore:

Michael Clarke

Since great Achilles and Atrides strove,
Such was the sovereign doom, and such the will of Jove!

POPE, *Iliad*, Book I.

The heavenly goddess here invoked was Calli'ope, the patroness of epic song, and one of the nine Muses. These were sister deities, daughters of Jupiter, who presided over poetry, science, music, and dancing. Apollo, as god of music and the fine arts, was their leader. They held their meetings on the top of Mount Par-nas'sus in Greece. On the slope of this mount was the celebrated spring or fountain of Cas-ta'li-a, whose waters were supposed to give the true poetic spirit to all who drank of them.

The epic poets usually began their poems by invoking the aid of the Muse. Homer does this in the very first line of the Iliad, the word for word translation of which is: "O goddess, sing the wrath of Achilles, the son of Peleus."

So also the English poet, Milton, begins his great epic poem, "Paradise Lost," which tells about the disobedience of Adam and Eve in the Garden of Eden:

Of man's first disobedience, and the fruit
Of that forbidden tree whose mortal taste
Brought death into the world, and all our woe,
With loss of Eden, till one greater Man
Restore us, and regain the blissful seat,
Sing, heavenly Muse, that, on the secret top
Of Oreb or of Sinai, didst inspire
That shepherd who first taught the chosen seed
In the beginning how the heavens and earth
Rose out of Chaos; or, if Sion hill
Delight thee more, and Siloa's brook that flow'd
Fast by the oracle of God, *I thence*
Invoke thy aid to my advent'rous song.

VI. THE DREAM OF AGAMEMNON

Very soon great evils came upon the Greeks because of the strife between the chiefs. When Chryseis was restored to her father, Apollo stopped the plague; but the wrong done to Achilles provoked the anger of another deity. This was Thetis, who, having much power with Jupiter, was able to persuade him to take up the cause of her injured son.

For as soon as the heralds departed from his tent, leading away the fair-cheeked Briseis, Achilles withdrew from his friends, retired to the seashore, and sitting there alone he bitterly wept, and with outstretched hands prayed to his mother, Thetis. The goddess heard his voice, and ascending from the depths of the ocean, where she dwelt in the palace of her aged father, Nereus, she sat down beside the hero, and soothing him with her hand, she inquired the cause of his distress. "Why do you weep, my son? What grief has come upon thy mind?"

Then Achilles related to his mother what Agamemnon had done, and he begged her to go to Mount Olympus and entreat Jupiter to punish the insult that had been offered to her son. He spoke of the service she had done for Jupiter long before, when Juno, Neptune, and Minerva had made a plot to bind him, and cast him from the throne of heaven. They might have succeeded in doing this if Thetis had not called Bri'a-reus up from Pluto's kingdom to help Jupiter. Briareus was a mighty giant who had a hundred hands, and his appearance in Olympus so terrified the conspirators that they did not attempt to carry out their wicked plot.

"Now," said Achilles to his mother, "remind Jupiter of this, and beg him to aid the Trojans and give them victory in battle, so that Agamemnon may feel the effects of his folly in dishonoring me."

"Ascend to heaven and bring thy prayer to Jove,
If e'er by word or act thou gav'st him aid.
For I remember, in my father's halls
I often heard thee, glorying, tell how thou,
Alone of all the gods, didst interpose
To save the cloud-compeller, Saturn's son,
From shameful overthrow, when all the rest
Who dwell upon Olympus had conspired
To bind him,—Juno, Neptune, and with them
Pallas Athene. Thou didst come and loose
His bonds, and call up to the Olympian heights
The hundred-handed, whom the immortal gods
Have named Briareus."

BRYANT, *Iliad*, Book I.

Thetis readily consented to do as her son desired.

"Not now, however!" said she, "for yesterday Jupiter went to E-thi-o'pi-a to a banquet, and all the gods went with him. But in twelve days he will return. Then I will go to Olympus and tell your words to thunder-delighting Jove, and I think I shall be able to persuade him to grant your request."

"Thou, meanwhile, abide
By thy swift ships, incensed against the Greeks,
And take no part in all their battles more."

BRYANT, *Iliad*, Book I.

Thetis did not forget her promise. On the twelfth day, at the dawn of morning, she emerged from beneath the waves, and went up to Olympus. There she threw herself at the feet of Jupiter, as he sat on the summit of the mount apart from the other gods, and earnestly prayed him to grant victory to the Trojans until the Greeks should make amends to her son for the injury that had been done him.

Now it may seem that it was not just to ask that the whole Greek army should be punished for the act of their general. But the other chiefs and their people were hardly less to blame than Agamemnon, for they did not try to prevent him from doing the wrong. If they had opposed him very much, he would not perhaps have dared to insult their greatest warrior, the man without whose help they knew Troy could not be taken. Therefore Thetis begged Jupiter to punish all the Greeks by giving victory to the Trojans.

> "O Jupiter, my father, if among
> The immortals I have ever given thee aid
> By word or act, deny not my request.
> Honor my son whose life is doomed to end
> So soon; for Agamemnon, king of men,
> Hath done him shameful wrong: he takes from him
> And keeps the prize he won in war. But thou,
> Olympian Jupiter, supremely wise,
> Honor him thou, and give the Trojan host
> The victory, until the humbled Greeks
> Heap large increase of honors on my son."

BRYANT, *Iliad*, Book I.

Jupiter hesitated for some time before consenting to grant the prayer of Thetis.

Michael Clarke

"This," said he, "is a serious matter, for by doing as you desire I may give offense to Juno, who has already been blaming me among the gods, saying that I aid the Trojans in battle. However, since you will have it so, I shall grant your request."

> "And that thou
> Mayst be assured, behold, I give the nod;
> For this, with me, the immortals know, portends
> The highest certainty; no word of mine
> Which once my nod confirms can be revoked,
> Or prove untrue, or fail to be fulfilled."

BRYANT, *Iliad*, Book I.

The awful nod was then given, and mighty Olympus trembled. Thetis, rejoicing at the success of her mission, departed from the heavenly regions and plunged into the depths of the sea, while Jupiter went to his golden palace where the other gods were sitting around the banqueting table. As he entered all rose up to do him honor, and met him as he advanced to his throne. But his talk with Thetis had not escaped the notice of Juno, and suspecting what it was about, she addressed her spouse in harsh words.

"Thou art ever," said she, "plotting secret things apart from me, and now I greatly fear that the silver-footed Thetis has persuaded thee to do some evil to the Greeks."

> "Thou hast promised her, I cannot doubt,
> To give Achilles honor and to cause
> Myriads of Greeks to perish by their fleet."

BRYANT, *Iliad*, Book I.

"You are always suspecting," answered Jupiter, "but now it will avail you nothing. Even though I have done what you say, such is my sovereign pleasure. Be silent, and sit down in peace, and take care not to provoke my anger."

At this point Vulcan interfered, entreating his mother, Juno, to submit to the will of almighty Jove; "for," said he, "if the Thunderer wishes to hurl us from our seats in heaven he can easily do it, since his power is far greater than that of all the other gods."

Vulcan then reminded her how she and he had both been punished on a former occasion for an offense against Jupiter. When Hercules was returning to Greece from Troy after capturing that city, Juno, who hated the great hero, caused a storm to be raised in the Ægean Sea, which drove his ships out of their course and almost destroyed them. That she might do this without Jupiter knowing it, she contrived to cast him into a deep sleep. When he awoke and found out what she had done, he was so angry that he hung her from the heavens by a golden chain, and tied two heavy iron anvils to her feet. Vulcan tried to loose the chains and set his mother free, and for this offense Jupiter hurled him from the abode of the gods. He fell on the island of Lem'nos in the Ægean Sea, but some of the inhabitants, seeing him descend, caught him in their arms. Nevertheless, he broke his leg by the fall and was ever afterwards lame.

> How he fell
> From heaven they fabled, thrown by angry Jove
> Sheer o'er the crystal battlements; from morn
> To noon he fell, from noon to dewy eve,
> A summer's day; and with the setting sun
> Dropped from the zenith, like a falling star,
> On Lemnos, the Ægean isle.

MILTON, *Paradise Lost*, Book I.

After reminding Juno of these things, and restoring peace

Michael Clarke

between her and the king of heaven, Vulcan took upon himself the office of cupbearer. He poured nectar into golden goblets and served it round to the gods and goddesses, all of whom laughed at the sight of the lame god bustling through the banqueting hall performing the work of Ganymede. They feasted till sunset, Apollo giving them sweet music from his lyre, while the goddesses of song accompanied him with their voices.

> Thus the blest gods the genial day prolong,
> In feasts ambrosial, and celestial song.
> Apollo tuned the lyre; the Muses round
> With voice alternate aid the silver sound.

POPE, *Iliad*, Book I.

When the banquet was over, the gods and goddesses retired to their palaces,—golden palaces built by Vulcan,—and they sought repose in sleep. But Jupiter did not sleep, for he was thinking how he might carry out his promise to Thetis. After much thought he resolved to send a message to Agamemnon by means of a dream, telling him to lead his forces at once against Troy, as it was the will of the gods that the city should now fall into the hands of the Greeks. And so this false Dream or Lying Spirit was sent on its deceitful errand. It took the form of the venerable Nestor, and, appearing to Agamemnon while he was sleeping in his tent, delivered to him the command of Jupiter:

> "Monarch, awake! 'tis Jove's command I bear;
> Thou and thy glory claim his heavenly care.
> In just array draw forth the embattled train,
> Lead all thy Grecians to the dusty plain;
> E'en now, O king! 'tis given thee to destroy
> The lofty towers of wide-extended Troy."

POPE, *Iliad*, Book II.

As soon as Agamemnon awoke he hastily called a council of the chiefs to meet at the ships of Nestor. There he told them of the command of Jove, as sent to him in his dream. All agreed that the divine will should be obeyed, but Agamemnon, like a prudent general, thought it would be well, before going to battle, to find out whether the troops, after their toils of nine years, were still willing to support him in carrying on the war. With this object he resolved to try the plan of pretending to them that he had made up his mind to stop the siege and return at once to Greece. But he directed the chiefs to advise their followers not to consent to the proposal, and to encourage them to make one more fight for the honor of their country. Then the heralds summoned the whole army to assemble, and the vast host gathered together on the plain before the camp, to listen to the words of their commander. Homer's description of the muster of the forces on this occasion is very beautiful:

> The sceptred rulers lead; the following host,
> Pour'd forth by thousands, darkens all the coast.
> As from some rocky cleft the shepherd sees
> Clustering in heaps on heaps the driving bees,
> Rolling and blackening, swarms succeeding swarms,
> With deeper murmurs and more hoarse alarms;
> Dusky they spread, a close embodied crowd,
> And o'er the vale descends the living cloud.
> So, from the tents and ships, a lengthen'd train
> Spreads all the beach, and wide o'ershades the plain:
> Along the region runs a deafening sound;
> Beneath their footsteps groans the trembling ground.

POPE, *Iliad*, Book II.

The whole Greek army being thus assembled, with the exception of the wrathful Achilles and his Myrmidons, Agamemnon then addressed them, leaning on his scepter. He told them he now believed that Troy could not be taken, and

Michael Clarke

that Jupiter, who before promised victory to the Greeks, now commanded them to return to Argos.

"Let us therefore," said he, "get ready our ships and hasten to set sail for our dear native land, where our wives with our beloved children sit within their dwellings expecting us." The proposal was received with a loud shout of joy, and the moment the king finished speaking, the vast multitude began at once to make preparations for launching the vessels into the sea.

> So was the whole assembly swayed; they ran
> With tumult to the ships; beneath their feet
> Rose clouds of dust, and each exhorted each
> To seize the ships and drag them to the deep.

BRYANT, *Iliad*, Book II.

But Juno, from her seat on high Olympus, was watching these movements, and she resolved that the war against the hated Trojans should not thus come to an end. She therefore sent Minerva down with a message to Ulysses. The azure-eyed goddess, as Minerva is often called by Homer, hastened to the Grecian camp, and approached the Ithacan king, who was standing near his ships, much grieved at seeing his countrymen preparing to depart. Minerva addressed him in earnest words, begging him to use his influence with the Greeks and persuade them not to go.

"It cannot be," said she, "that you, brave chiefs, will leave to Priam the glory of victory, and to the Trojans possession of Helen, on whose account so many of your people have perished, far from their native land."

Ulysses knew the voice of the goddess, and promptly he complied with her request. He went among the ships and talked to the leaders, reminding them that it was not

Agamemnon's wish that they should give up the war, and entreating them to set an example of courage to their followers.

"Warriors like you, with strength and wisdom bless'd,
By brave examples should confirm the rest."

POPE, *Iliad*, Book II.

He also spoke to the soldiers, reproving them for their hasty flight, and bidding them listen to the words of their leaders, who knew better than they when and how to act. His efforts were successful. As speedily as they had fled to their ships the Greeks now rushed back, and again assembled to await the orders of their commander.

Back to the assembly roll the thronging train,
Desert the ships, and pour upon the plain.

POPE, *Iliad*, Book II.

But there was one evil-minded individual who tried to incite the others to rebellion. This was Ther-si'tes, a vulgar brawler, and the ugliest man in the whole Greek army.

Of the multitude
Who came to Ilium, none so base as he,—
Squint-eyed, with one lame foot, and on his back
A lump, and shoulders curving towards the chest;
His head was sharp, and over it the hairs
Were thinly scattered.

BRYANT, *Iliad*, Book II.

This ill-conditioned grumbler, as deformed in mind as in body, took much pleasure in abusing the bravest warriors of the army, particularly Achilles and Ulysses. But on the

Michael Clarke

present occasion he raised his shrill voice in words of insult against Agamemnon. "Your tents," cried he to the king, "are full of money and prizes bestowed upon you by us. Do you want still more gold, which we by our valor must win for you from the enemy? If the Greeks were not women instead of men, they would return home in their ships and leave you here to fight the Trojans. Little honor and few prizes would you then have!"

"O ye coward race!
Ye abject Greeklings, Greeks no longer, haste
Homeward with all the fleet, and let us leave
This man at Troy to win his trophies here."

BRYANT, *Iliad*, Book II.

Thus did Thersites revile Agamemnon, but his insolent speech brought speedy punishment upon him. Ulysses, who was close at hand, turned with angry looks upon the offender and rebuked him in stern language. Then with his scepter he smote Thersites on the back and shoulders, until he wept with pain and crouched down upon his seat in fear and trembling.

Trembling he sat, and shrunk in abject fears,
From his vile visage wiped the scalding tears.

POPE, *Iliad*, Book II.

All the Greeks laughed heartily at the cowering wretch as he wiped his face, and they loudly applauded the act of the Ithacan chief. "Surely," said they, "Ulysses has performed many good deeds, but now he has done the best thing of all in punishing this foul-mouthed reviler as he deserved."

Then Ulysses, taking in his hand the famous scepter of Agamemnon, made an eloquent speech to the army,

Minerva, the azure-eyed, in the appearance of a herald, having commanded the people to be silent, that they might hear the words of the wisest of their leaders. It was upon this occasion that the Ithacan king told the story of the serpent devouring the birds at Aulis, as already related. Many of the Greeks had forgotten the marvelous occurrence, and the prediction of Calchas that in the tenth year of the siege Troy would be taken. Being now reminded of it, they were filled with fresh hope and courage, for the tenth year had come, and the end of the contest was not far off, which was to be for them a great victory, as the soothsayer had declared. "Therefore, brave Greeks," said Ulysses, after telling the story, "since the prophecy is so near its fulfillment, let us all remain here until we have captured the city of Priam."

> He spake, and loud applause thereon ensued
> From all the Greeks, and fearfully the ships
> Rang with the clamorous voices uttering
> The praises of Ulysses, and his words.

BRYANT, *Iliad*, Book II.

The venerable Nestor and King Agamemnon then addressed the troops, after which they all went to their tents and ships to prepare for battle. They began by making the customary sacrifices to the gods, Agamemnon offered up a fat ox five years old. Homer fully describes how this was done. First the king and his chiefs stood around the ox, holding pounded barley cakes in their upraised hands, and praying to Jupiter to grant them victory in the approaching battle. After the prayer the ox was killed, and the carcass cut into pieces. Portions of the flesh were then burned on leafless billets, while other portions were roasted for the banquet which followed.

After the banquet the loud-voiced heralds summoned all the warriors and their followers to assemble. Immediately they came from their ships and tents, and then, on the advice of

Michael Clarke

Nestor, there was a review of the whole army. The azure-eyed Minerva moved amongst them, bearing in her hand the ægis, or shield of Jupiter, from which hung a hundred golden fringes, each "worth a hundred oxen in price." She went through the hosts of the Greeks encouraging them to fight bravely, and so they were now more eager for battle than to return to their native land.

It is at this part of his story—the review of the forces—that Homer gives the remarkable account known as the "Catalogue of the Ships." In it he tells the names of all the Greek kings and princes and chiefs, the Grecian states from which they came, and the number of ships which each brought to the war. To do this was no easy task, and so the poet, before undertaking it, again seeks the aid of the Muses:

> O Muses, goddesses who dwell on high,
> Tell me,—for all things ye behold and know,
> While we know nothing and may only hear
> The random tales of rumor,—tell me who
> Were chiefs and princes of the Greeks; for I
> Should fail to number and to name them all,—
> Had I ten tongues, ten throats, a voice unapt
> To weary, uttered from a heart of brass,—
> Unless the Muses aided me.

BRYANT, *Iliad*, Book II.

The allies and leaders of the Trojans are also named and described in the "Catalogue of the Ships," for they too were marshaling their forces within the city. From their walls they had observed the movements of the Greeks, and, moreover, Jupiter had sent down his swift-footed messenger, I'ris, to bid them get ready for battle. The goddess found Priam and Hector and others of the chiefs of Troy sitting in council, and she told them of the vast host of the Greeks that was just then marching towards the city.

"I have seen many battles, yet have ne'er
Beheld such armies, and so vast as these,—
In number like the sands and summer leaves.
They march across the plain, prepared to give
Battle beneath the city walls. To thee,
O Hector, it belongs to heed my voice
And counsel. Many are the allies within
The walls of this great town of Priam, men
Of diverse race and speech. Let every chief
Of these array his countrymen for war,
And give them orders for the coming fight."

BRYANT, *Iliad*, Book II.

Hector promptly obeyed the command of the goddess.
Dismissing the council, he and the other chiefs at once
placed themselves at the head of their troops and marched
forth through the gates into the plain.

Michael Clarke

VII. THE COMBAT BETWEEN MENELAUS AND PARIS

The two great armies, now in battle array on the plain before the city walls, began to advance towards each other. The Trojans moved along with great clatter, which Homer compares to the noise of flocks of cranes:

> The Trojan host moved on
> With shouts and clang of arms, as when the cry
> Of cranes is in the air, that, flying south
> From winter and its mighty breadth of rain,
> Wing their way over ocean.

BRYANT, *Iliad*, Book III.

The Greeks, on the other hand, advanced in deep silence.

> But silently the Greeks
> Went forward, breathing valor, mindful still
> To aid each other in the coming fray.
> As when the south wind shrouds a mountain-top
> In vapors that awake the shepherd's fear,—
> A surer covert for the thief than night,—
> And round him one can only see as far
> As one can hurl a stone,—such was the cloud
> Of dust that from the warriors' trampling feet
> Rose round their rapid march and filled the air.

BRYANT, *Iliad*, Book III.

As soon as the armies approached each other, almost front to front, Paris rushed forward from the Trojan lines, and challenged the Greeks to send their bravest warrior to fight him in simple combat. In appearance he was beautiful as a god. Over his shoulders he wore a panther's skin. His weapons were a bow, a sword, and two spears tipped with brass, which he brandished in his hands. The challenge was speedily answered by Menelaus, who bounded from his chariot the moment he beheld Paris, rejoicing that at last the time had come to have revenge on the man who had so greatly wronged him.

> As a hungry lion who has made
> A prey of some large beast—a horned stag
> Or mountain goat—rejoices, and with speed
> Devours it, though swift hounds and sturdy youths
> Press on his flank, so Menelaus felt
> Great joy when Paris, of the godlike form,
> Appeared in sight, for now he thought to wreak
> His vengence on the guilty one, and straight
> Sprang from his car to earth with all his arms.

BRYANT, *Iliad*, Book III.

But when Paris saw who it was that had come forth to fight him, he was seized with a great fear, and he shrank back into the ranks of his companions.

> As one who meets within a mountain glade
> A serpent, starts aside with sudden fright, ·
> And takes the backward way with trembling limbs.

BRYANT, *Iliad*, Book III.

Michael Clarke

Though Paris was really a brave man, his feeling of his own guilt and the sight of Menelaus, whom he had injured, made him a coward for the moment, and so he fled from before the face of the enraged king of Sparta. The noble Hector was deeply vexed at seeing his brother's flight, and in angry words upbraided him for his shameful conduct.

"Better would it have been," said he, "if you had never been born than thus to bring disgrace upon us all. Well may the Greeks laugh at finding that you, whom they supposed to be a hero, possess neither spirit nor courage. You have brought evil on your father, your city, and your people, by carrying away a beautiful woman from her husband, yet you now fear to meet that warrior in battle. The Trojans are but a weak-minded race, else they would have long since given you the death you deserve."

Paris admitted that his brother's rebuke was just, and he now declared that he was willing to meet Menelaus in single combat, Helen and her treasures to be the prize of the victor.

"Cause the Trojans and the Greeks
To pause from battle, while, between the hosts,
I and the warlike Menelaus strive
In single fight for Helen and her wealth.
Whoever shall prevail and prove himself
The better warrior, let him take with him
The treasure and the woman, and depart;
While all the other Trojans, having made
A faithful league of amity? shall dwell
On Ilium's fertile plain, and all the Greeks
Return to Argos."

BRYANT, *Iliad*, Book III.

Hector rejoiced at his brother's words, and, immediately going forward into the center of the open space between the two armies, he spoke in a loud voice to the Greeks and Trojans, telling them of the proposal which Paris had made. The brave Menelaus heard the challenge with delight, and promptly accepted it.

> "Now hear me also,—me whose spirit feels
> The wrong most keenly. I propose that now
> The Greeks and Trojans separate reconciled,
> For greatly have ye suffered for the sake
> Of this my quarrel, and the original fault
> Of Paris. Whomsoever fate ordains
> To perish, let him die; but let the rest
> Be from this moment reconciled, and part."

BRYANT, *Iliad*, Book III.

The Greeks and Trojans were happy at the hope thus offered of a speedy end to the war. Hector sent for King Priam, that he and Agamemnon and the other leaders on both sides might declare their approval of the proposed conditions, and pledge themselves in the presence of both armies to abide by the result of the combat between the two heroes. Just then the Trojan monarch was seated on one of the watchtowers of the walls, looking down on the plain where the great hosts were assembled. With him were several of his venerable chiefs, now too old to take part in fighting.

While they sat there the beautiful Helen came out from the palace to witness the approaching conflict. She had been told of it by the messenger Iris, who, descending from heaven, and taking the form of La-od'i-ce, one of Priam's daughters, appeared to Helen in her chamber. There she was busy at her loom, making in golden tapestry a representation of some of the great events of the war. In those days, as we read in many parts of Homer, the noblest ladies, even queens and their daughters, did not think it beneath them to work at spinning and weaving and other useful occupations, and so Helen was

Michael Clarke

employed when Iris came to tell her that Paris and Menelaus were about to fight for her and her treasure.

From her spinning Helen rose up and went to the walls to view the combat. As she came near the place where Priam sat, even the venerable chiefs were compelled to admire her wondrous beauty. "Fair as the immortal goddesses she is," said they; "yet much better would it be if she would return to her own country, and not remain here to bring ruin upon us and our children." But Priam called to her to sit by his side, and said to her:

> "No crime of thine our present sufferings draws,
> Not thou, but Heaven's disposing will, the cause
> The gods these armies and this force employ,
> The hostile gods conspire the fate of Troy."

POPE, *Iliad*, Book III.

Then King Priam asked Helen to name for him some of the Greek leaders whom he saw before him, not far from the city walls.

"Who is that tall and gallant hero," he asked, "who seems like unto a king? Never have I beheld a man so graceful, nor so venerable." "Revered and honored father," answered Helen, "would that death had taken me before I left my husband and home to come with your son hither, but the Fates did not will it so, therefore am I here. That hero whom you see is the wide-ruling Agamemnon, the son of Atreus, both a good king and a brave warrior, and once my brother-in-law."

> "My brother once, before my days of shame,
> And oh! that still he bore a brother's name!"

POPE, *Iliad*, Book III.

"O happy Agamemnon," exclaimed Priam, "fortunate in ruling over so mighty a host! But who is this other chief, less in height than Agamemnon, though broader in the shoulders? His arms lie on the ground, while he himself moves from rank to rank like a thick-fleeced ram which wanders through a great flock of sheep."

"The stately ram thus measures o'er the ground,
And, master of the flock, surveys them round."

POPE, *Iliad*, Book III.

"That," said Helen, "is the wise Ulysses, man of many arts. Though nursed in a rugged island, yet is he skilled in all kinds of stratagem and prudent counsel." Ajax and Idomeneus were next noticed by King Priam,—Ajax the mighty, who overtopped the Argives by his head and shoulders, and Idomeneus the valiant king of Crete. Helen knew them well, for she had seen them at her Spartan home.

"Ajax the great," the beauteous queen replied,
"Himself a host; the Grecian strength and pride.
See! bold Idomeneus superior towers
Amid yon circle of his Cretan powers,
Great as a god! I saw him once before,
With Menelaus on the Spartan shore.
The rest I know, and could in order name;
All valiant chiefs, and men of mighty fame."

POPE, *Iliad*, Book III.

But at this point the heralds sent by Hector came to tell Priam that he was wanted on the plain below to approve the terms of the challenge. Immediately the king, descending from the ramparts, mounted his chariot, accompanied by his wise counselor, Antenor. They drove through the Scæan Gate into the space between both armies, and there, with the

Michael Clarke

ceremonies usual on such occasions, a solemn league was formed between the two monarchs. First, they mixed in a bowl wine brought by both parties. This was an emblem of reconciliation. Next, water was poured on the hands of the kings, after which Agamemnon cut with his dagger hairs from the heads of three lambs. These were divided among the chiefs on both sides, so that all might be bound by the pledge about to be made. Then Agamemnon, stretching forth his hands, prayed thus aloud:

"O father Jupiter, most glorious, most mighty, and thou, O Sun, who beholdest all things, and ye rivers, and thou earth, and ye in the regions of the dead that punish those who swear false oaths, be ye witnesses of this league. If, on the one hand, Paris slay Menelaus, let him keep Helen and all her possessions, and let us return home in our ships. But if, on the contrary, Menelaus slay Paris, let the Trojans restore Helen and all her treasures, and pay a fine to the Argives such as may be just."

Then the lambs were sacrificed, and the kings drank of the mixed wine. Some of it was also poured on the earth, while the Greeks and Trojans joined in praying that terrible punishment might be sent upon any person who should violate the league:

"Hear, mighty Jove! and hear, ye gods on high!
And may their blood, who first the league confound,
Shed like this wine, disdain the thirsty ground."

POPE, *Iliad*, Book III.

Such was the league formed between the kings and chiefs of the two great armies. Priam then went back to the city, for he could not bear to witness a conflict in which his son might be slain. Lots were now drawn to decide which of the warriors should cast his spear first. Paris won, and immediately the champions, putting on their armor and taking up their weapons, advanced into the middle of the ground that Hector and Ulysses had measured out for the combat.

Then the fight began. Paris hurled his javelin, but Menelaus warded off the blow with his strong brazen shield. In his turn the Spartan king poised his long spear for a throw at his enemy. At the same time he prayed to Jupiter to give him strength and victory:

> "O Sovereign Jove! vouchsafe that I avenge
> On guilty Paris wrongs which he was first
> To offer; let him fall beneath my hand,
> That men may dread hereafter to requite
> The friendship of a host with injury."

BRYANT, *Iliad*, Book III.

Then Menelaus cast his spear. It pierced the shield and corselet of Paris, and might have made a fatal wound had he not bent himself sideways, and so escaped the full force of the weapon. Instantly Menelaus rushed forward, sword in hand, and dealt a powerful blow at his enemy's head. This time Paris was saved by the brazen helmet he wore, for when Menelaus struck it, the blade of his sword broke in pieces.

Angry at his ill luck, the Spartan warrior seized his foe by the horsehair crest of his helmet, and began to drag him towards the Grecian lines; but at this point Venus came to the aid of her favorite. Standing unseen beside him, she broke the helmet strap under his chin, and thus released him from the grasp of the wrathful Menelaus. Then she cast a thick mist around the Trojan prince, and, carrying him off to the city, set him down in his chamber, within his own palace. The goddess also conducted Helen to the palace, from the watchtower in which, after her conversation with Priam, she had remained to witness the combat on the plain. As soon as

Michael Clarke

Helen beheld Paris she spoke to him in harsh words:

"Com'st thou from battle? Rather would that thou
Hadst perished by the mighty hand of him
Who was my husband. It was once, I know,
Thy boast that thou wert more than peer in strength
And power of hand, and practice with the spear,
To warlike Menelaus. Go then now,
Defy him to the combat once again.
And yet I counsel thee to stand aloof,
Nor rashly seek a combat, hand to hand,
With fair-haired Menelaus, lest perchance
He smite thee with his spear and thou be slain."

BRYANT, *Iliad*, Book III.

Meanwhile the Spartan king, furious as a lion, paced up and
down the field searching for Paris, but not even the Trojans
could tell where he was. If he were amongst them they
would not have concealed him, for they loved him not,
knowing that he was the cause of all the sufferings which the
long war had brought upon them.

None of all
The Trojans, or of their renowned allies,
Could point him out to Menelaus, loved
Of Mars; and had they known his lurking-place
They would not for his sake have kept him hid,
For like black death they hated him.

BRYANT, *Iliad*, Book III.

Paris having disappeared from the field, the Greeks claimed
the victory for their champion, and Agamemnon called upon
the Trojans to give up Helen and her treasures, in accordance
with the conditions of the league. But the gods did not thus
will it. The Fates had decreed the destruction of Troy, and so

the war could not have a peaceful ending. Besides, the Greeks were doomed to suffer as Jupiter had promised Thetis, because of the wrong that had been done to Achilles. Therefore, after the matter had been discussed in a council of the gods in their golden palace on Olympus, Minerva was sent down to urge the Trojans to attack the Greeks, so that the league might be broken, and the war renewed. According to the custom of heavenly messengers in such cases, the goddess took the form of La-od'o-cus, son of Antenor. Then, approaching Pan'da-rus, a famous archer of the Trojan allies, she persuaded him to aim an arrow at Menelaus.

"Great honor," she said, "you will have from all the Trojans, if you slay the son of Atreus, and from Paris you may expect splendid gifts."

But Minerva, being friendly to the Greeks, did not really wish that Menelaus should be killed; therefore, when Pandarus bent his bow and with true aim let fly his arrow, she took care to turn the deadly weapon aside.

Pallas assists, and (weakened in its force)
Diverts the weapon from its destined course:
So from her babe, when slumber seals his eye,
The watchful mother wafts the envenom'd fly.

POPE, *Iliad*, Book IV.

Nevertheless the arrow pierced the Spartan king's belt and made a slight wound, but the skillful surgeon, Ma-cha'on, son of the famous physician, Æsculapius, stanched the blood and applied soothing balsams which his father had taught him to use.

The league being thus broken by the treacherous act of Pandarus, both sides at once prepared for battle. Agamemnon went on foot through his army, speaking words

Michael Clarke

of praise to the chiefs, whom he found active in marshaling and encouraging their men. "Father Jupiter," he said, "will not help those Trojans who have so basely broken their solemn pledges. When we have taken their city we shall carry away rich spoils in our ships." Of all the leaders none arranged and directed his troops more wisely than the venerable Nestor.

> The cavalry with steeds and cars he placed
> In front. A vast and valiant multitude
> Of infantry he stationed in the rear,
> To be the bulwark of the war. Between
> He made the faint of spirit take their place,
> That, though unwillingly, they might be forced
> To combat with the rest.

BRYANT, *Iliad*, Book IV.

Then he gave strict orders to the charioteers, warning them not to trust too much to their valor, or rashly advance in front of their comrades.

> "Let no man, too vain of horsemanship,
> And trusting in his valor, dare advance
> Beyond the rest to attack the men of Troy,
> Nor let him fall behind the rest, to make
> Our ranks the weaker. Whoso from his car
> Can reach an enemy's, let him stand and strike
> With his long spear, for 'tis the shrewder way."

BRYANT, *Iliad*, Book IV.

VIII. THE FIRST GREAT BATTLE

Nearly three books of the Iliad are occupied in telling about the battle that now followed, though it lasted only one day. But it was a fierce and mighty conflict in which many brave warriors fought and fell.

> For that day
> Saw many a Trojan slain, and many a Greek,
> Stretched side by side upon the bloody field.

BRYANT, *Iliad*, Book IV.

All the chiefs of both armies took part in this battle, except Achilles, who still remained inactive at his ships, "indignant for the sake of the fair-haired Briseis." The heroes of the day on the Trojan side were Hector and Æneas. Of the Greeks (also sometimes called A-cha'ians) none performed so many feats of valor as Diomede (or Diomed), also called Ty-di'des, from the name of his father, Ty'deus. He was the particular favorite of Minerva, who caused a bright light to shine from his shield and helmet, which made him a striking figure in the field, and very terrible to the enemy.

> Pallas to Tydides Diomed
> Gave strength and courage, that he might appear
> Among the Achaians greatly eminent,
> And win a glorious name. Upon his head

And shield she caused a constant flame to play,
Like to the autumnal star that shines in heaven
Most brightly when new-bathed in ocean tides.
Such light she caused to beam upon his crest
And shoulders, as she sent the warrior forth
Into the thick and tumult of the fight.

BRYANT, *Iliad*, Book V.

Diomede slew many brave warriors, and often, breaking through the close ranks of the Trojans, drove them back towards their walls, before he himself was smitten with an arrow sent flying at him by the archer Pandarus. The weapon pierced his shoulder right through, and the blood came streaming down his armor. Then Pandarus shouted to his comrades to advance, boasting that now the bravest of the Greeks was fatally wounded. But Diomede prayed to Minerva for aid, and his prayer was heard. Immediately the goddess appeared and stood beside him, and in an instant healed his wound. Then she encouraged him, saying: "Henceforth fight with confidence, O Diomede. I have given you great strength. I have also removed from your eyes the mortal mists which heretofore were upon them, so that now you may know gods from men. Beware, however, of using your weapons against any god, unless Venus should come into the battle. Her I desire and command you to wound."

With fresh courage and increased fury Diomede again rushed into the conflict, striking down a Trojan with every blow of his huge sword. Æneas, noticing his exploits, hastily sought out Pandarus and begged him to aim an arrow at the man who was thus destroying their ranks.

"That man," said Pandarus, "very much resembles the warlike son of Tydeus, and if it be he, some god is surely at his side to protect him, for only a little ago I smote him in the shoulder, and I thought I had sent him to Pluto's kingdom. Of small use it seems is this bow of mine. Already I have aimed at two chiefs, Menelaus and Diomede, and wounded both, but I have only roused them the more to heroic deeds."

"In an evil hour
I took my bow and quiver from the wall
And came to lead the Trojans for the sake
Of Hector. But if ever I return
To see my native country and my wife
And my tall spacious mansion, may some foe
Strike off my head if with these hands I fail
To break my bow in pieces, casting it
Into the flames, a useless weapon now."

BRYANT, *Iliad*, Book V.

But Æneas made the great archer try his skill once more. Taking Pandarus with him in his own chariot, he drove rapidly to where Diomede was dealing death amongst the Trojans with his terrible sword. Sthen'e-lus, the companion and charioteer of Diomede, saw them coming, and he advised his friend to retreat, and not risk his life in a contest with two such heroes as Æneas and Pandarus, one the son of a goddess, and the other excelling all men in the use of the bow. But Diomede sternly refused to retire from the conflict. Nor would he even consent to mount his chariot as Sthenelus urged him to do.

"As I am," said he, "I shall advance against them, for Minerva has made me fearless. And if it be my fortune to slay both, do you, Sthenelus, seize the horses of Æneas and drive them into the ranks of the Greeks. Valuable prizes they will be, for they are of that heavenly breed which Jupiter gave to King Tros as the price of his son Ganymede."

But now the chariot of Æneas was close at hand. This time Pandarus used his spear, which he launched with great force.

Michael Clarke

It struck the shield of Diomede and, piercing it through, fixed itself in his breastplate. With a shout of joy Pandarus exclaimed, "Now, I think, I have given you your death wound."

"Not so," replied the son of Tydeus, "thou hast missed thy aim, but one of you, at least, shall die." As he spoke he hurled his lance. Directed by Minerva, the weapon flew right into the face of the unfortunate Pandarus, striking him lifeless to the earth.

> Headlong he falls, his helmet knocks the ground;
> Earth groans beneath him, and his arms resound.

POPE, *Iliad*, Book V.

Instantly Æneas leaped down from his chariot, with his shield and spear, to defend the body of his heroic comrade against being despoiled by the Greeks. This was one of the customs of war in those times. When a hero was slain in battle the enemy carried off his arms and armor as trophies of victory. But Æneas did his best to protect the corpse of his fallen friend from being thus dishonored.

> Watchful he wheels, protects it every way,
> As the grim lion stalks around his prey.
> O'er the fall'n trunk his ample shield displayed,
> He hides the hero with his mighty shade,
> And threats aloud! the Greeks with longing eyes
> Behold at distance, but forbear the prize.

POPE, *Iliad*, Book V.

But Diomede, braver than the rest, took up a great stone and hurled it at Æneas.

Not two strong men the enormous weight could raise,
Such men as live in these degenerate days.

POPE, *Iliad*, Book. V.

It struck the Trojan hero on the hip, tearing the flesh and
crushing the joint. He sank upon his knees, a dark mist
covering his eyes. And now Æneas would have perished by
the sword of the furious Diomede had not his mother, Venus,
come quickly to his aid. With her shining robe the goddess
shielded his body, and spreading her arms about him she
bore him away from the battle. Then Sthenelus, not
forgetting the bidding of his friend, rushed forward, and,
seizing the fleet steeds of the Dardan prince, drove them off
to the Grecian camp.

But Diomede went in pursuit of Venus. He had seen and
recognized her as she descended on the field, Minerva
having given him power of sight to know gods from men.
The goddess also, as we have seen, commanded him to
wound Venus should she come into the field. Diomede,
therefore, when he had overtaken Venus, as she was bearing
away the Trojan hero, thrust at her with his lance, and
pierced the skin of her tender hand. From the wound out
gushed the I'chor, as the blood of the gods was called.

The ichor,—such
As from the blessed gods may flow; for they
Eat not the wheaten loaf, nor drink dark wine;
And therefore they are bloodless, and are called
Immortal.

BRYANT, *Iliad*, Book V.

Crying aloud with pain, the goddess dropped her son from
her arms, but Apollo enveloped him in a thick cloud, thus
saving him from the wrath of the furious Greeks. Meanwhile

Michael Clarke

the swift-footed Iris hastened down from heaven to the aid of Venus, whom she conducted to where Mars sat on the left of the battlefield, watching the conflict. At the entreaty of his wounded sister.

> Mars resigned to her his steeds
> With trappings of bright gold. She climbed the car,
> Still grieving, and, beside her, Iris took
> Her seat, and caught the reins and plied the lash.
> On flew the coursers, on, with willing speed,
> And soon were at the mansion of the gods
> On high Olympus.

BRYANT, *Iliad*, Book V.

There the goddess was affectionately received by her mother, Di-o'ne, who begged her to be patient, reminding her that in times past others of the gods had suffered by the hands of men. Mars, she said, was chained in a brazen cell for fifteen months by the giants O'tus and Eph-i-al'tes, and he would perhaps have perished there but that Mercury set him free by stealing into the cell, and slipping the chains out of the rings to which they were fastened. Juno herself, and Pluto, the god of Hades, were wounded by Hercules. "As for this son of Tydeus," said Dione, "who has dared to war upon an immortal, he shall be punished for his crime."

> "The fool!
> He knew not that, the man who dares to meet
> The gods in combat lives not long. No child
> Shall prattling call him father when he comes
> Returning from the dreadful tasks of war."

POPE, *Iliad*, Book V.

Dione then wiped the ichor from the hand of Venus, and at her touch the wound healed and the pain ceased.

Meanwhile, on the plain before Troy Diomede still eagerly pursued Æneas, though knowing that the hero was under divine protection. Thrice did he rush on, and thrice did Apollo drive him back, but when he made the fourth attempt,

> The archer of the skies, Apollo, thus
> With menacing words rebuked him: "Diomed,
> Beware; desist, nor think to make thyself
> The equal of a god. The deathless race
> Of gods is not as those who walk the earth."

BRYANT, *Iliad*, Book V.

Diomede shrank back, fearing the wrath of the Far-darter, and Apollo bore Æneas away, and set him down in his own temple in sacred Per'ga-mus, the citadel of Troy. There Diana and La-to'na, the mother of Apollo, healed his wound and restored his health and strength. Then Apollo begged Mars to assist the Trojans in the battle, and particularly to drive from the field the impious son of Tydeus, who had dared to attack the immortals with his spear, and would now fight even with Jupiter himself. The god of war consented, and assuming the form of Ac'a-mas, a Thracian leader, he went through the Trojan ranks encouraging the chiefs to fight bravely.

> "O sons of Priam, him who claims descent
> From Jupiter! how long will ye submit
> To see your people slaughtered by the Greeks?
> Is it until the battle-storm shall reach
> Your city's stately portals?"

POPE, *Iliad*, Book V.

The hero Sarpedon also appealed to Hector, and then the Trojan commander in chief, leaping from his chariot, and brandishing his javelins, rushed among his troops exhorting them to battle.

> Terrible
> The conflict that ensued. The men of Troy
> Made head against the Greeks: the Greeks stood firm,
> Nor ever thought of flight.

BRYANT, *Iliad*, Book V.

Soon, however, the Greeks were forced to fall back. Their great chiefs, Agamemnon and Menelaus, and the two Ajaxes and Ulysses, performed wondrous deeds of courage, slaying many Trojan warriors. But Minerva had left the field, and Mars was fighting on the Trojan side. Æneas, too, had returned to the battle with renewed strength and courage, and Hector and Sarpedon were in the front, dealing death among the enemy. The fierce god of war and mighty Hector fought side by side, and they slew numbers of Argive warriors.

Such destruction of her beloved Greeks was not pleasing to Juno, who was watching the conflict from her place on high Olympus, and she begged of Jupiter to permit her to drive Mars from the battle. Jupiter consented, but he advised her to intrust that work to Minerva, who had often before "brought grievous troubles on the god of war." Juno obeyed. Then the two goddesses, who had already mounted the queen of heaven's own grand chariot, glittering with gold and silver and brass, set out for the Grecian camp.

> Eight brazen spokes in radiant order flame;
> The circles gold, of uncorrupted frame,
> Such as the heavens produce: and round the gold
> Two brazen rings of work divine were roll'd.
> The bossy naves of solid silver shone;
> Braces of gold suspend the moving throne;
> The car, behind, an arching figure bore;
> The bending concave form'd an arch before.

Silver the beam, the extended yoke was gold,
And golden reins the immortal coursers hold.

POPE, *Iliad*, Book V.

Riding in this magnificent chariot, driven by Juno herself,
"midway between the earth and the starry heaven," the
goddesses descended upon the plain of Troy, near where the
Simois and the Scamander united their streams. There they
alighted, and cast a dense mist around the chariot and the
steeds to hide them from mortal view. Then they hastened to
where the bravest of the Greek chiefs were standing around
the warrior Diomede, Juno likening herself to the herald
Sten'tor, who had a voice louder than the shout of fifty men.

Stentor the strong, endued with brazen lungs,
Whose throat surpass'd the force of fifty tongues.

POPE, *Iliad*, Book V.

Appearing before the Greek chiefs in the form of the loud-
voiced herald, the queen of heaven cried out in words of
reproof:

"Shame upon you, Argives! You are heroes only in name.
While the divine Achilles was with you, fighting at the front,
the Trojans dared not advance beyond their gates, for they
dreaded his mighty spear; but now they are almost at your
ships."

Minerva, too, severely censured Diomede for holding back
from the battle, but the warrior answered that it was by her
command that he had refrained from attacking Mars. "You
did not permit me," said he, "to fight with any of the gods
except Venus."

"Fear not this Mars at all," answered Minerva, "nor any of

Michael Clarke

the immortals. Come now and direct your steeds against the war god, and I will be with you." So saying, and putting on her head the helmet of Pluto, which made any person who wore it invisible, she mounted the chariot beside the brave Diomede, and, seizing the reins, drove rapidly to where the fierce Mars was slaying Greek warriors.

As soon as Mars beheld Diomede approaching, he rushed against him, and hurled his brazen spear; but Minerva grasped the weapon and turned it aside from the chariot. Diomede now thrust forward his lance, Minerva directing it, and adding her strength to give force to the blow. It pierced the loin of the war god, making a deep wound.

Mars bellows with the pain:
Loud as the roar encountering armies yield,
When shouting millions shake the thundering field.
Both armies start, and trembling gaze around;
And earth and heaven rebellow to the sound.

POPE, *Iliad*, Book V.

The wounded god disappeared in a dark cloud, and, quickly ascending to Olympus, made bitter complaint to Jupiter against Minerva. But the king of heaven sternly reproved him, saying that he had brought his sufferings upon himself, for discord and wars were always his delight. Nevertheless he ordered Pæ'on, the physician of the gods, to heal the wound, which was immediately done.

Meanwhile Juno and Minerva returned to Olympus, Mars being removed from the battlefield. And now the fortune of war began to favor the Greeks. The Trojans, no longer aided by a god fighting on their side, were driven back to their walls, and it seemed as if they were about to be totally defeated. In this perilous situation Helenus, the prophet and soothsayer, advised his brother Hector to go quickly into the city, and request their mother, the queen, to call together the matrons of Troy, and with them to offer up sacrifices and prayers in the temple of Minerva, begging the help and protection of that goddess. The advice seemed good to Hector. Leaping from his chariot, he went through the army bidding the warriors to fight bravely during his absence. Then he hastened to the city. At the Scæan Gate he was met by crowds of anxious wives and mothers and daughters, who eagerly inquired for their husbands, sons, and brothers.

> He admonished all
> Duly to importune the gods in prayer,
> For woe, he said, was near to many a one.

BRYANT, *Iliad*, Book VI.

Arriving at the royal palace Hector was met by his mother, who offered him wine to refresh himself with. But the hero would not taste the liquor. "Do not ask me to drink wine, dear mother," he said, "for it would enfeeble me, and deprive me of my strength and valor."

> "Inflaming wine, pernicious to mankind,
> Unnerves the limbs, and dulls the noble mind."

POPE, *Iliad*, Book VI.

Then Hector told his mother why he had come from the field of battle. She gladly consented to do as her son requested, and so Queen Hecuba and the matrons of Troy went to the temple of Minerva, and prayed and offered sacrifices. But the goddess refused to hear their prayers, for she still hated the Trojans because of the never-forgotten judgment on Mount Ida.

Meantime the hero went to the palace of Paris, whom he found in his chamber, handling and preparing his armor, while Helen sat near him with her maids, directing their various tasks. Angry at seeing his brother thus engaged, instead of being in the front of the fight, Hector reproached him in sharp and bitter words.

"The people," said he, "are perishing, the conflict rages round the walls, and all on your account. Arise, then, and act, lest our city soon be in flames." Paris answered mildly, saying that he deserved his brother's censure, and promising that he would immediately repair to the field of battle.

Hector next proceeded to his own home to visit his dear wife, An-drom'a-che, and his infant son; "for I know not," said he, "whether I shall ever return to them again." Arriving at the palace, he learned from Andromache's maids that their mistress had just gone towards the city walls.

> "To the lofty tower of Troy she went
> When it was told her that the Trojan troops
> Lost heart, and that the valor of the Greeks
> Prevailed. She now is hurrying toward the walls.
> Like one distracted, with her son and nurse."

> BRYANT, *Iliad*, Book VI.

Leaving the palace, Hector hastened through the city, and, arriving at the Scæan Gate, he there met Andromache and her nurse, the latter bearing in her arms the infant Sca-man'dri-us. His father had given the child this name, from the name of the river, but the people called him As-ty'a-nax, meaning "city-king." The lines in which Homer describes the interview which here took place between the noble Hector and his loving wife, are among the most beautiful of the whole Iliad. Andromache was a daughter of E-ë'ti-on, king of Thebe, the town from which the maiden Chryseis was carried away. Eëtion and all his family had been slain, with the exception of Andromache, who therefore had now neither parents nor brothers nor sisters. Of this she spoke in touching words, while entreating Hector to remain within the city and not again risk his life in battle.

"Too brave! thy valor yet will cause thy death:
Thou hast no pity on thy tender child,
Nor me, unhappy one, who soon must be
Thy widow. All the Greeks will rush on thee
To take thy life. A happier lot were mine,
If I must lose thee, to go down to earth,
For I shall have no hope when thou art gone,—
Nothing but sorrow. Father I have none,
And no dear mother. Great Achilles slew
My father when he sacked the populous town
Of the Cilicians,—Thebe with high gates.
Hector, thou
Art father and dear mother now to me,
And brother and my youthful spouse besides.
In pity keep within the fortress here,
Nor make thy child an orphan nor thy wife   A widow."

BRYANT, *Iliad*, Book VI.

Hector was deeply moved by these words, but he could not think of deserting his brave companions.

"All this
I bear in mind, dear wife; but I should stand
Ashamed before the men and long-robed dames
Of Troy, were I to keep aloof and shun
The conflict, cowardlike. Not thus my heart
Prompts me, for greatly have I learned to dare
And strike among the foremost sons of Troy,
Upholding my great father's fame and mine;
Yet well in my undoubting mind I know
The day shall come in which our sacred Troy,
And Priam, and the people over whom

Spear-bearing Priam rules, shall perish all."

BRYANT, *Iliad*, Book VI.

But it was not the dark prospect of his country's ruin that grieved the loving husband so much as the thought that his wife might some day be carried off as a slave by the conquering Greeks.

"But not the sorrows of the Trojan race,
Nor those of Hecuba herself, nor those
Of royal Priam, nor the woes that wait
My brothers many and brave,—who all at last,
Slain by the pitiless foe, shall lie in dust,—
Grieve me so much as thine, when some mailed Greek
Shall lead thee weeping hence, and take from thee
Thy day of freedom. . . . .
O let the earth
Be heaped above my head in death before
I hear thy cries as thou art borne away!"

BRYANT, *Iliad*, Book VI.

Then Hector stretched out his hands to embrace his son, but the little fellow shrank back and screamed in fright at the nodding crest on his father's helmet. Both parents gently smiled, and Hector, taking off his helmet, and placing it on the ground, kissed his boy, and fondled him in his arms, praying to the gods that he might become a brave warrior, and the defender of his country.

"O Jupiter and all ye deities,
Vouchsafe that this my son may yet become
Among the Trojans eminent like me,
And nobly rule in Ilium. May they say,
'This man is greater than his father was.'"

BRYANT, *Iliad*, Book VI.

The parting between the hero and his sorrowing wife was very affecting. Andromache received the infant from his father's arms, mingling tears with her smiles as she looked into the face of her child.

> The chief
> Beheld, and, moved with tender pity, smoothed
> Her forehead gently with his hand and said:—
> "Sorrow not thus, beloved one, for me.
> No living man can send me to the shades
> Before my time; no man of woman born,
> Coward or brave, can shun his destiny.
> But go thou home, and tend thy labors there,—
> The web, the distaff,—and command thy maids
> To speed the work. The cares of war pertain
> To all men born in Troy, and most to me."

BRYANT, *Iliad*, Book VI.

Then Hector took his helmet from the ground, and Andromache departed for her home, "oft looking back, and shedding many tears."

As the hero went out at the Scæan Gate, after taking leave of his wife, he met Paris, arrayed in his shining armor, and eager to join the battle. Together they rushed into the plain, and slew many of the enemy. The goddess Minerva, observing that the battle was going against the Greeks, quickly descended from the top of Olympus. Apollo, seeing her from the Trojan citadel, hastened to meet her, and he proposed that they should now bring the conflict to an end for the day. With this object, Minerva having consented, they both agreed to cause Hector to challenge one of the Greek warriors to engage with him in single combat. Helenus, being a soothsayer, knew the purpose of the gods, and he told his brother. "But," said he, "you shall not fall in the fight, for it is not thy fate yet to perish. Thus have the immortal gods spoken, and I have heard their voice."

Hector rejoiced at his brother's words, and immediately advancing to the front of the army he commanded the Trojans to cease fighting.

He bore his spear,
Holding it in the middle, and pressed back
The ranks of Trojans, and they all sat down.
And Agamemnon caused the well-armed Greeks
To sit down also.

BRYANT, *Iliad*, Book VII.

Then the Trojan chief, standing between the two hosts, spoke in a loud voice, and challenged the bravest of the Greeks to engage with him in mortal combat. For a few moments there was silence in the ranks of the Argives. Even the boldest of them hesitated at the thought of fighting such a warrior as Hector. At length Menelaus, rising from his seat, declared that he was ready to accept the challenge, and so he put on his armor. But Agamemnon held him back, warning him against rashly venturing into a conflict with a man who was much stronger and braver than he, and whom every other chief, even Achilles himself, regarded with fear.

Nestor then arose, and in severe words upbraided his countrymen for their want of courage. "Would that my frame were unworn with years," he exclaimed, "then Hector should soon find a foe to meet him; but now among the bravest of the Achaians there is no one to meet the Trojan leader in arms."

The venerable Nestor had no sooner ceased speaking than nine warriors started to their feet, every one eager for the honor of being permitted to accept the challenge of Hector. Among them were Agamemnon, the two Ajaxes, Diomede, and Ulysses. Nestor then proposed that one should be chosen by lot. This was agreed to, and lots being cast, the honor fell to Ajax Telamon, the mightiest and most valiant of the Greeks except Achilles. The hero greatly rejoiced, believing that he would conquer Hector, and so he quickly put on his armor, and went forward to the ground marked out for the combat.

His massy javelin quivering in his hand,
He stood, the bulwark of the Grecian band.

POPE, *Iliad*, Book VII.

Hector having also taken his place on the ground, the combat began. First the Trojan chief, brandishing his long spear, hurled it at his foe. Ajax received it on his shield, which was made of seven folds of oxhides and an eighth fold of solid brass. Through six of the hides the weapon of Hector pierced, but it stuck fast in the seventh.

Then the Grecian champion sent forth his javelin. It passed right through Hector's shield and corselet, and might have proved fatal, had the hero not quickly bent aside his body. Again both champions launched spears, one after the other. This time Hector was slightly wounded in the neck. Nothing daunted, however, he seized a huge stone which lay at his feet, and hurled it at Ajax. It struck the hero's shield and the brass resounded with the blow. Quickly the Argive warrior took up a much larger stone, and flung it at his antagonist with tremendous force. The stone crashed through Hector's shield, and, striking him on the knee, stretched him flat on the ground. But Apollo instantly raised him up, renewing his strength, and then with their swords the two heroes fell upon each other, fighting hand to hand. At this point, night having come on, two heralds, one from the Trojan army, the other

Michael Clarke

from the Greek, approached the champions, and ordered them to cease fighting, I-dae'us, the Trojan herald, giving the command in a loud voice:

"Cease to contend, dear sons, in deadly fray;
Ye both are loved by cloud-compelling Jove,
And both are great in war, as all men know.
The night is come; be then the night obeyed."

BRYANT, *Iliad*, Book VII.

Ajax answered that as it was Hector who gave the challenge, it was for him first to speak of truce. Hector replied, speaking words of praise and admiration for his antagonist, and saying that they should now cease from battle for the day.

"Since, then, the night extends her gloomy shade,
And heaven enjoins it, be the night obey'd.
Return, brave Ajax, to thy Grecian friends,
And joy the nations whom thy arm defends;
But let us, on this memorable day,
Exchange some gift: that Greece and Troy may say
'Not hate, but glory, made these chiefs contend;
And each brave foe was in his soul a friend.'"

POPE, *Iliad*, Book VII.

Then Hector gave Ajax a silver-studded sword with scabbard, and Ajax presented to Hector a belt of rich purple. Thus ended the terrible conflict which had raged throughout the day, and the two heroes retired, each joyfully welcomed by his comrades and friends.

Then they both departed,—one
To join the Grecian host, and one to meet
The Trojan people, who rejoiced to see

Hector alive, unwounded, and now safe
From the great might and irresistible arm
Of Ajax. Straightway to the town they led
Him for whose life they scarce had dared to hope.
And Ajax also by the well-armed Greeks,
Exulting in his feats of arms, was brought
To noble Agamemnon.

BRYANT, *Iliad*, Book VII.

Michael Clarke

IX. THE SECOND BATTLE
—EXPLOIT OF DIOMEDE AND ULYSSES

Before the Greek leaders retired to rest for the night, they held a council in the tent of Agamemnon, at which they resolved to perform funeral rites, early in the morning, in honor of their comrades who had been slain in the battle. They also resolved, on the advice of Nestor, to build a strong wall and dig a deep trench in front of their camp, that their ships might be secure against the attacks of the enemy.

The Trojan chiefs, too, held a council. They were discouraged by their losses in the battle, and many of them thought that they could not now succeed in the war, because of the treacherous act of Pandarus in breaking the league. The wise Antenor was of this opinion, and in his speech at the council he advised that Helen and her treasures should be given up to the Greeks.

"Send we the Argive Helen back with all
Her treasures; let the sons of Atreus lead
The dame away; for now we wage the war
After our faith is broken, and I deem
We cannot prosper till we make amends."

BRYANT, *Iliad*, Book VII.

But Paris would not agree to this. He was willing to give up Helen's treasures, and to give treasure of his own as compensation to the Greeks, but he would not consent to restore Helen herself. King Priam weakly gave way to his son, and ordered that a herald should be sent to the Greek leaders to tell them of the offer of Paris, and to request that fighting should not be resumed until the dead should be taken from the battlefield, and funeral services performed.

Accordingly the Trojan herald Idæus went next morning to the tent of Agamemnon. There he found the Argive chiefs assembled. Upon hearing his message, they scornfully rejected the terms proposed by Paris, but they agreed to a truce for the funeral ceremonies. Idæus returned to the city, and told the Trojan leaders of the answer he had received. Both Greeks and Trojans then began collecting their dead from the field and building great piles of wood, or pyres, to burn the bodies upon.

> All wailing, silently they bore away
> Their slaughtered friends, and heaped them on the pyre
> With aching hearts, and, when they had consumed
> The dead with fire, returned to hallowed Troy.
> The nobly-armed Achaians also heaped
> Their slaughtered warriors on the funeral pile
> With aching hearts; and when they had consumed
> Their dead with fire they sought their hollow ships.

> BRYANT, *Iliad*, Book VII.

Before dawn next morning the Greeks set about building a wall and digging a trench on the side of their camp facing Troy, as Nestor had advised. They finished the work in one day, and a mighty work it was. The wall was strengthened with lofty towers, and the gates were so large that chariots could pass through. The trench was broad and deep, and on the outer edge it was defended by strong, sharp stakes. The

Michael Clarke

gods, looking down from Olympus, admired these labors, but Neptune, much displeased, made bitter complaint to Jupiter:

"Now will the fame
Of this their work go forth wherever shines
The light of day, and men will quite forget
The wall which once we built with toiling hands—
Phœbus Apollo and myself—around
The city of renowned Laomedon."

BRYANT, *Iliad*, Book VII.

But Jupiter relieved the anxiety of the ocean god by telling him that when the war was over, and the Greeks had departed from Troy, he might overthrow the great wall with his waves, and cover the shore with sand. Thus the Grecian bulwark would vanish from the plain.

After their great labors on the wall and trench the Greeks feasted in their tents, and next day, the truce being now ended, both armies prepared for battle. Meanwhile Jupiter, held a council on high Olympus, at which he gave strict command that none of the gods should take part on either side in the fight before Troy; and he declared that if any of them should disobey this order, he would hurl the offender down into the dark pit of Tar'ta-rus, in the gloomy kingdom of Pluto.

Deep, deep in the great gulf below the earth,
With iron gates and threshold forged of brass.

BRYANT, *Iliad*, Book VIII.

But Minerva begged that she might be permitted to assist the Greeks by her advice. To this the king of heaven assented. Then mounting his chariot, to which were yoked his brazen-footed, swift-flying steeds, adorned with golden manes, he sped through the skies between the earth and starry heaven to the summit of Mount Ida. There in a sacred inclosure in which was an altar erected to him, the father of the gods sat looking down upon the towers of Ilium and the ships of the Greeks. The two hosts, led by their great chiefs, were now engaged in fierce battle.

> The sounding darts in iron tempests flew;
> Victors and vanquish'd join promiscuous cries,
> Triumphant shouts and dying groans arise;
> With streaming blood the slippery fields are dyed,
> And slaughtered heroes swell the dreadful tide.

POPE, *Iliad*, Book VIII.

Thus the terrible conflict went on until midday, when Jupiter, taking in his hand the golden scales of fate, weighed the fortunes of the Trojans and Greeks.

> By the midst
> He held the balance, and, behold, the fate
> Of Greece in that day's fight sank down until
> It touched the nourishing earth, while that of Troy
> Rose and flew upward toward the spacious heaven.

BRYANT, *Iliad*, Book VIII.

Then the mighty god thundered from Mount Ida, and sent his lightnings burning and flashing down against the army of the Greeks. In amazement and terror the Argive chiefs fled from the field. Nestor alone remained, though not willingly, for he too was seeking safety in flight when one of the horses of his chariot was killed by an arrow from the bow of Paris. The venerable king himself might have perished at the hands of Hector, had not Diomede hastened up and taken him into his own chariot.

Both warriors then advanced against the Trojan chief, and Diomede hurled his javelin. The weapon missed Hector, but killed his charioteer. Still rushing on, the brave son of Tydeus was about to cast another spear, when a terrific bolt of lightning flashed from the heavens and tore up the earth in front of his steeds. Looking upon this as a sign of the anger of Jupiter, the two heroes hastily retreated towards their camp. Hector pursued them, and the Trojans, encouraged by his example, now pressed forward until the Greeks were driven in behind their trench and wall. Then Agamemnon, in deep despair, prayed to almighty Jove that he would at least permit him and his people to get away in safety with their ships.

"Now be at least one wish of mine fulfilled,—
That we may yet escape and get us hence;
Nor let the Trojans thus destroy the Greeks."

BRYANT, *Iliad*, Book VIII.

Jupiter heard the prayer of the king, and in pity for his distress sent a favorable omen. This was an eagle bearing in its talons a fawn, which it dropped down by the side of the altar where the Greek chiefs were just then offering sacrifice. Believing that the bird had come from Jove, the Greeks took courage, and rushing out through their gates, with Diomede and Agamemnon and Menelaus and Ajax at their head, they furiously attacked the Trojans and slew many of them. Teucer, the brother of Ajax Telamon, did great destruction with his bow and arrows, in the use of which he was as skillful even as Pandarus. After killing several of the enemy, he aimed twice at Hector, missing him, however, each time, but at the second shot he slew the Trojan leader's charioteer. Hector then jumped to the ground, and, seizing a great stone, hurled it with mighty force, striking the unfortunate Teucer on the neck, and felling him to the earth. And now the Trojans, rushing once more upon the Greeks, again drove them back to their camp.

> They drave
> The Achaians backward to the yawning trench.
> Then Hector came, with fury in his eyes,
> Among the foremost warriors. As a hound,
> Sure of his own swift feet, attacks behind
> The lion or wild boar, and tears his flank,
> Yet warily observes him as he turns,
> So Hector followed close the long-haired Greeks,
> And ever slew the hindmost as they fled.

BRYANT, *Iliad*, Book VIII.

But night now put an end to the battle. This was a most welcome relief to the Greek leaders, thoroughly disheartened as they were at the sight of the enemy almost at their ships. On the other hand the warriors of Troy "most unwillingly beheld the sunset," for it prevented them from following up their victory. But Hector was confident that on the next day he would be able to destroy the Achaian host and fleet, and so end the war. He therefore addressed his troops, commanding them to remain on the field for the night, that they might be ready to fall upon the Greeks, should they attempt to go aboard their vessels, and "escape across the mighty deep."

> So high in hope, they sat the whole night through
> In warlike lines, and many watch fires blazed.

BRYANT, *Iliad*, Book VIII.

Meanwhile the Grecian leaders held a council of war, and Agamemnon advised that they should take to their ships, and set sail for Greece, as it now seemed to be the will of Jupiter that they should never capture Troy. Upon hearing this the chiefs sat for a time in gloomy silence. At length Diomede

Michael Clarke

spoke out, censuring the king for his cowardly counsel.

"The gods," said he, "have given you, O son of Atreus, high rank and great power, but not much of courage. Return home if you are so inclined, but the other Greeks will remain until they have overthrown Troy, for it was by the direction of the immortals that we came here."

These words were loudly applauded by the assembled leaders. Then guards were placed to watch the wall and trench, after which Agamemnon gave the chiefs a banquet in his tent. When all had partaken of the good things set before them, the wise Nestor advised that an effort be made to appease the anger of Achilles. This proposal even Agamemnon warmly approved, for he now admitted that he had done a great wrong in taking away Briseis, and he declared that he would restore the maiden at once to Achilles, and send him rich gifts besides.

> "I erred, and I deny it not.
> That man indeed is equal to a host,
> Whom Jupiter doth love and honor thus,
> Humbling the Achaian people for his sake.
> And now, since, yielding to my wayward mood
> I erred, let me appease him, if I may,
> With gifts of priceless worth."

> BRYANT, *Iliad*, Book IX.

Agamemnon then promised that he would send to Achilles a large sum in gold, with twenty shining caldrons, and twelve steeds which had won many prizes by their fleetness. Moreover, when they should return to Greece after having conquered the Trojans, he would give him one of his daughters to be his wife, and with her, as a marriage portion, seven rich cities of Argos.

The Greek chiefs were very glad to hear these proposals, and they resolved to appoint ambassadors to send to Achilles to beg him to accept these gifts and make peace with Agamemnon. On the advice of Nestor they chose for this important mission the prudent Ulysses, an aged chief named Phœ'nix, and the valiant warrior Ajax. Phœnix had been the instructor of Achilles in his youth, and had been sent by King Peleus with the expedition to Troy to be his son's friend and counselor. The three ambassadors, with two heralds, accordingly set out for the camp of the Myrmidonian chief. They found him sitting in his tent with his friend Patroclus.

> Amused at ease, the godlike man they found,
> Pleased with the solemn harp's harmonious sound.
> (The well wrought harp from conquered Thebæ came;
> Of polish'd silver was its costly frame).
> With this he soothes his angry soul, and sings
> The immortal deeds of heroes and of kings.

POPE, *Iliad*, Book IX.

The ambassadors were received with great respect. Achilles rose from his seat and welcomed them as warriors and friends. Then food and drink were placed before them, and after they had refreshed themselves, Ulysses stated the object of their visit. He described the danger of the Grecian army, threatened with destruction by the terrible Hector and his victorious hosts. He next told of the many gifts which Agamemnon had offered, and then in earnest words he begged Achilles to lay aside his anger, and come to the relief of his countrymen in their great peril.

But the wrath of the son of Peleus was not thus to be appeased. He replied to Ulysses in a long speech, recounting his services during the war, and bitterly complaining of the ingratitude and selfishness of Agamemnon.

Michael Clarke

"Twelve cities have I with my fleet laid waste,
And with my Myrmidons have I o'erthrown
Eleven upon this fertile Trojan coast.
Full many a precious spoil from these I bore,
And to Atrides Agamemnon gave.
He, loitering in his fleet, received them all;
Few he distributed, and many kept."

BRYANT, *Iliad*, Book IX.

As for the apologies which Agamemnon now made, the
wrathful hero declared that he could have no confidence in a
man who had deceived him, nor would he accept the offered
gifts.

"Let him ne'er again,
Though shameless, dare to look me in the face.
I will not join in council nor in act
With him: he has deceived and wronged me once,
And now he cannot wheedle me with words.
Let once suffice. I leave him to himself,
To perish. All-providing Jupiter
Hath made him mad. I hate his gifts; I hold
In utter scorn the giver."

BRYANT, *Iliad*, Book IX.

In vain also were the entreaties of Phœnix and Ajax. They
too tried to persuade the hero to dismiss from his mind the
thought of his wrongs, and lead his brave Myrmidons once
more into the field for the honor of his country. But Achilles
persisted in his refusal to take further part in the war, and so
there was nothing left for the ambassadors but to return to
the tent of Agamemnon and report the failure of their mission.

In deep disappointment and distress the chiefs heard the
story. Then again they held counsel together to consider

what was best to do,—whether to prepare for another battle, or to betake themselves at once to their ships and set sail for Greece. Nestor proposed that some brave and prudent chief should venture into the Trojan camp, and, if possible, find out what were the plans of Hector.

> "Is there (said he) a chief so greatly brave,
> His life to hazard, and his country save?
> Lives there a man, who singly dares to go
> To yonder camp, or seize some straggling foe?
> Or favor'd by the night approach so near,
> Their speech, their counsels, and designs to hear?"

POPE, *Iliad*, Book X.

Diomede offered himself for this service, and being permitted to select a companion, he made choice of Ulysses. The two warriors at once put on their armor, and took up their weapons. Then they went out into the plain, each praying to Minerva to grant them success. Cautiously they moved forward towards the camp of the enemy.

> With dreadful thoughts they trace the dreary way,
> Through the black horrors of the ensanguined plain,
> Through dust, through blood, o'er arms, and hills of slain.

POPE, *Iliad*, Book X.

Now it happened that about the same time Hector had sent a young Trojan chief, Do'lon by name, on a similar errand,—to make his way into the Grecian camp, and find out the designs of the Argive leaders. Dolon offered to undertake the dangerous task on condition that he should have as his reward the chariot and horses of Achilles, when the Greeks should be conquered. Hector agreed to the condition, and the Trojan spy, arming himself, set forth for the Greek camp. He had not gone far when Ulysses and Diomede saw him

Michael Clarke

advancing, whereupon they lay down among the dead bodies and allowed him to go forward a considerable distance. Then they rose up and followed him.

At first Dolon supposed that they were Trojans sent by Hector to call him back, but, soon seeing that they were enemies, he fled with great speed in the direction of the ships. The two Greeks hastened in pursuit, and Diomede hurled a spear after the fugitive. He purposely missed him, however, for their object was to take the Trojan alive, that they might get from him the information they desired. The weapon passed over the shoulder of Dolon, and sank into the ground in front of him. Instantly he stood still, trembling with fear, and the Greek warriors, hurrying up, seized him by the hands. The frightened Trojan flung himself on his knees, and begged them to spare his life, promising that his father, who was rich, would pay a high ransom. Ulysses commanded him to tell what his errand was to the Grecian camp, and also to tell them all about the Trojan army, and of the plans of Hector.

"Tell me,—and tell the truth,—where hast thou left
Hector, the leader of the host, and where
Are laid his warlike arms; where stand his steeds;
Where are the sentinels, and where the tents
Of other chiefs? On what do they consult?
Will they remain beside our galleys here,
Or do they meditate, since, as they say,
The Greeks are beaten, a return to Troy?"

BRYANT, *Iliad*, Book X.

The terrified Dolon, hoping to move the Greeks to mercy, told even more than he was asked to tell. There was a Thracian king, he said, who had that very day arrived with a troop of soldiers to help the Trojans. Rhe'sus was his name. He had steeds beautiful to behold, and fleet as the wind, his chariot shone with gold and silver, and the armor he wore was all of gold.

"Even now," said Dolon, "Rhesus and his followers are in a camp by themselves separated from the others, and it will be easy to take them by surprise as they lie asleep, and carry off the rich things they possess."

This news was joyfully received by the Greek heroes. They had heard of an oracle which declared that Troy could never be captured if these same horses of Rhesus should once drink of the water of Xanthus or feed on the grass of the Trojan plain. They therefore resolved to rob Rhesus of his magnificent steeds. But first they killed the unhappy Dolon, paying no heed to his prayers for mercy. Then they hurried on to the Thracian camp, where they found the warriors sunk in deep repose, after the fatigues of the day's journey.

> There slept the warriors, overpowered with toil;
> Their glittering arms were near them, fairly ranged
> In triple rows, and by each suit of arms
> Two coursers. Rhesus slumbered in the midst.
> Near him were his fleet horses, which were made
> Fast to the chariot's border by the reins.

BRYANT, *Iliad*, Book X.

Diomede slew Rhesus and twrelve of his companions, while Ulysses untied the king's steeds, and led them forth into the field. Then, hastening across the plain with their rich prize, they soon reached the Grecian camp, where Nestor and the other chiefs joyfully welcomed them.

> Their friends, rejoicing, flocked
> Around them, greeting them with grasp of hands
> And with glad words.

BRYANT, *Iliad*, Book X.

X. THE BATTLE AT THE SHIPS —DEATH OF PATROCLUS

At dawn the Achaian leaders resolved to try again the fortunes of war. They were encouraged by the exploit of Ulysses and Diomede, and Jupiter sent down Eris, the goddess of strife, to incite them to ardor for battle. The goddess stood on the ship of Ulysses, which was in the center of the fleet, and shouted so loud that she was heard all over the Greek camp.

> Loud was the voice, and terrible, in which
> She shouted from her station to the Greeks,
> And into every heart it carried strength,
> And the resolve to combat manfully,
> And never yield. The battle now to them
> Seemed more to be desired than the return
> To their dear country in their roomy ships.

BRYANT, *Iliad*, Book XI.

Then began the greatest battle of the siege. So numerous were the exploits of heroes in this mighty conflict that the account of it occupies nearly eight books of the Iliad.

Agamemnon led the Grecian warriors during the earlier part of the day. He was arrayed in brilliant armor, his breastplate being of gold and bronze and tin.

Ten were its bars of tawny bronze, and twelve
Were gold, and twenty tin; and on each side
Were three bronze serpents stretching toward the neck.

BRYANT, *Iliad*, Book XI.

His sword, glittering with golden studs, hung from his shoulder in a silver sheath, and in his hands he bore two great spears, brass-tipped and sharp. As he went forth to meet the foe, Juno and Minerva made a sound as of thunder in the sky, "honoring the king of Mycenæ, rich in gold." Thus did the Argive chief enter the field at the head of his warriors.

The Trojans were already on the ground, their great leader, Hector, clad in shining brazen armor, giving his commands, now in the front and now in the rear. Like wolves rushing to combat the two hosts sprang against each other, and soon the battle raged furiously, the heroes on both sides fighting with equal valor.

They of Troy
And they of Argos smote each other down,
And neither thought of ignominious flight.

BRYANT, *Iliad*, Book XI.

But about midday the Greeks prevailed against the Trojans, and drove them back to the city gates. Agamemnon slew with his sword two of King Priam's sons, I'sus and An'ti-phus, and with his spear he struck down many of the Trojan heroes.

Hector had not yet taken part in the battle; Jupiter having sent him an order by the messenger Iris not to begin fighting until Agamemnon should retire wounded from the field. This soon happened. The king was wounded in the arm by the

Trojan chief Co'on, whose brother, I-phid'a-mas, Agamemnon had slain. These two chiefs were sons of the venerable Antenor. But Agamemnon, before withdrawing, rushed upon Coön and slew him also. Then, leaping into his chariot, he ordered his charioteer to drive him quickly to his ships, for he was suffering much from the pain of his wound.

Hector, seeing the flight of the Greek leader, called loudly to the Trojans to advance upon their foes, at the same time setting them the example.

> Himself, inspired
> With fiery valor, rushed among the foes
> In the mid-battle foremost, like a storm
> That swoops from heaven, and on the dark-blue sea
> Falls suddenly, and stirs it to its depths.

> BRYANT, *Iliad*, Book XI.

The fortune of battle now turned in favor of the men of Troy. Nine warrior princes of the Greeks were struck down, one after another, by the sword of Hector. The brave Diomede, wounded by an arrow from the bow of Paris, was obliged to retire to his tent. A spear hurled by the Trojan chief, So'cus, pierced the corselet of Ulysses, and wounded him in the side. But the Trojan did not long survive this exploit, for as he turned to flee, Ulysses sent a javelin through his body, felling him lifeless to the earth. A serious misfortune had almost happened to the Greeks at the hand of Paris, who shot a triple barbed arrow at the hero and physician, Machaon, wounding him in the shoulder. The life of the great son of Æsculapius being worth many men, Idomeneus cried to Nestor to come and take him away in his chariot.

> "Haste, mount thy chariot; let Machaon take
> A place beside thee; urge thy firm-paced steeds
> Rapidly toward the fleet; a leech like him,

Who cuts the arrow from the wound and soothes
The pain with balms, is worth a host to us."

BRYANT, *Iliad* Book XI.

Many of their leaders being now disabled, the Greeks were
driven from the field and forced to take refuge behind their
fortifications. At the trench a terrible conflict took place. The
Trojan warriors made efforts to pass it in their chariots, while
the Greeks fought with desperate fury to force the invaders
back. Many heroes on both sides were wounded and many
slain.

The towers and battlements were steeped in blood
Of heroes,—Greeks and Trojans.

BRYANT, *Iliad*, Book XII.

At last Hector took up a large stone and hurled it with
tremendous force against one of the gates. It tore off the
strong hinges, and shattered the massive beams, so mighty
was the blow. Then through the wide opening the Trojan
leader sprang into the Grecian camp, brandishing two spears
in his hands, and calling on his men to follow. Promptly they
obeyed. Some rushed in by the gateway, and some over the
wall, while the terrified Greeks fled in disorder and dismay
to their ships.

So far none of the gods had taken part in the battle. But
Neptune now resolved to come to the rescue of the Greeks,
having observed that Jupiter, though still seated in his sacred
inclosure on Mount Ida, was no longer watching the conflict.

On Troy no more
He turned those glorious eyes, for now he deemed
That none of all the gods would seek to aid
Either the Greeks or Trojans in the strife.

BRYANT, *Iliad*, Book XIII.

The ocean god, however, resolved to make the attempt. From the wooded height of Samothrace he had been viewing the fight, and had seen that the Achaian army and fleet were threatened with destruction. Quickly, therefore, descending to the sea, he plunged down to his golden mansion beneath the waves, and there put on his armor and mounted his chariot.

> He yoked his swift and brazen-footed steeds,
> With manes of flowing gold, to draw his car,
> And put on golden mail, and took his scourge,
> Wrought of fine gold, and climbed the chariot-seat,
> And rode upon the waves. The whales came forth
> From their deep haunts, and frolicked round his way:
> They knew their king. The waves rejoicing smoothed
> A path, and rapidly the coursers flew;
> Nor was the brazen axle wet below.
> And thus they brought him to the Greecian fleet.

BRYANT, *Iliad*, Book XIII.

Arrived at the fleet, Neptune assumed the shape and voice of the soothsayer Calchas, and, going amongst the Grecian leaders, urged them to battle. With his scepter he touched the two Ajaxes, thereby giving more than mortal strength to their limbs, and filling their breasts with valor. Thus encouraged the Greek heroes turned fiercely upon the Trojans, and again great feats of war were performed by the chiefs on both sides. Hector, Paris, Helenus, Deiph'o-bus, and Æneas fought in front of the Trojan lines, while Menelaus, Idomeneus, Teucer, the two Ajaxes, and An-til'o-chus, the son of Nestor, bravely led the conflict at the head of the Greeks.

> All along the line
> The murderous conflict bristled with long spears.

BRYANT, *Iliad*, Book XIII.

Juno rejoiced exceedingly at seeing the monarch of the ocean aiding the Greeks, but she much feared that Jupiter might notice him, and order him off the field. This he would be sure to do, if he should again turn his eyes on the battle. Juno therefore went to the island of Les'bos, where Som'nus, the god of sleep, resided, and she entreated that deity to hasten to Mount Ida, and cause her royal spouse to fall into a deep slumber. Somnus consented, and having done as Juno desired, he hurried down to the Grecian fleet with a message to Neptune.

> "Now, Neptune, give the Greeks thy earnest aid,
> And though it be but for a little space,
> While Jupiter yet slumbers, let them win
> The glory of the day; for I have wrapt
> His senses in a gentle lethargy."

BRYANT, *Iliad*, Book XIV.

Hearing these words, Neptune rushed to the front of the Greek lines and again urged the leaders to stand bravely against the enemy. Then, grasping in his hand a sword "of fearful length and flashing blade like lightning," he led them on to battle.

And now the warriors of both sides were once more in deadly conflict. Hector cast a spear at Ajax, but the weapon struck where two belts crossed upon the hero's breast, overlapping each other, and he escaped unhurt. Then the son of Telamon struck at the Trojan leader. His weapon was a heavy stone, one of many that lay around, which were used as props for the ships. The missile, hurled with giant force and true aim, smote the Trojan on the breast and felled him like a tree struck by lightning.

Michael Clarke

As when beneath
The stroke of Father Jupiter an oak
Falls broken at the root, ...
So dropped the valiant Hector to the earth
Amid the dust; his hand let fall the spear;
His shield and helm fell with him, and his mail
Of shining brass clashed round him.

BRYANT, *Iliad*, Book XIV.

With shouts of triumph the Greeks rushed forward, hoping to slay the fallen warrior, and despoil him of his armor. But his comrades, Æneas and A-ge'nor and Sarpedon and many others, crowded around him, and protected him with their shields. He was then carried to the bank of the Xanthus and bathed in its waters, which revived him a little.

When the Greeks saw Hector borne away as if dead, they fought with increased valor, and soon drove the Trojans back across the trench, slaying many of their chiefs.

Meanwhile Jupiter, awaking from his slumber, and looking down upon the battlefield, beheld the men of Troy put to flight, and Neptune at the head of the pursuing Greeks. Turning angrily upon Juno, who was at his side, he rebuked her in severe words, for he now saw the trick that had been played upon him. He reminded her of how he had punished her on a former occasion for her ill treatment of his son Hercules.

"Dost thou forget
When thou didst swing suspended, and I tied
Two anvils to thy feet, and bound a chain
Of gold that none could break around thy wrists?
Then didst thou hang in air amid the clouds,
And all the gods of high Olympus saw
With pity. They stood near, but none of them

Were able to release thee."

BRYANT, *Iliad*, Book XV.

Juno pleaded that it was not at her request that Neptune had gone to the aid of the Greeks. He had done that without consulting her. She indeed, she said, would rather advise Neptune to obey the command of the king of heaven and submit to his will.

The anger of the father of the gods was appeased by Juno's mild words. Then he bade her hasten to Olympus and send the messenger Iris down to order Neptune to leave the battle. He bade her also to direct Apollo to restore Hector's strength and prepare him for the fight. But he explained to Juno why he wished that for the present the Trojans should be victorious. It was because he had promised Thetis that the Greeks should be punished for the wrong Agamemnon had done to her son. Yet the time would come, he said, when the great Hector would be slain by the hand of Achilles, and when by Minerva's aid the lofty towers of Troy would be overthrown. Juno was therefore glad to obey the command of her royal spouse.

> As the thought of man
> Flies rapidly, when, having traveled far,
> He thinks, "Here would I be, I would be there,"
> And flits from place to place, so swiftly flew
> Imperial Juno to the Olympian mount.

BRYANT, *Iliad*, Book XV.

There she informed Iris and Apollo of the will of Father Jove. Forthwith the two gods hastened to Mount Ida to receive their orders from Jupiter himself. The orders were quickly given. Then with the speed of the winds the messenger of heaven and the god of the silver bow darted down from Ida's top to the plain of Troy.

Neptune, on hearing of the command of Jupiter, was at first unwilling to obey. Jupiter, he said, had no authority over him.

"We are three brothers,
The sons of Saturn,—Jupiter and I,
And Pluto, regent of the realm below.
Three parts were made of all existing things,
And each of us received his heritage.
The lots were shaken; and to me it fell
To dwell forever in the hoary deep,
And Pluto took the gloomy realm of night,
And lastly, Jupiter the ample heaven
And air and clouds. Yet doth the earth remain,
With high Olympus, common to us all.
Therefore I yield me not to do his will,
Great as he is; and let him be content
With his third part."

BRYANT, *Iliad*, Book XV.

But Iris advised Neptune to obey, reminding him that Jupiter had power of punishing those who offended him. At last Neptune yielded, and, quitting the Grecian army, took his way to the sea, and plunged beneath the waves to his palace in the ocean depths.

Meanwhile Apollo hastened to the side of the Trojan prince, who was still weak from the blow of Ajax. Quickly the god restored the hero's strength and breathed fresh courage into his breast. Then he commanded Hector to hasten forward and lead his warriors against the enemy. In an instant the Trojan prince was on his feet, hurrying to the front. When the Greek chiefs saw him they were astonished as well as terrified, for they had thought him dead, and now they believed he had been rescued from death by some god. They resolved, however, to fight bravely, and so they stood firmly together. Hector meanwhile advanced, Apollo moving before him with the shield of Jupiter, the terrible aegis, which Jupiter had given him to shake before the Greeks and fill their hearts with fear.

> "Hector led
> The van in rapid march. Before him walked
> Phœbus, the terrible aggis in his hands,
> Dazzlingly bright within its shaggy fringe,
> By Vulcan forged, the great artificer,
> And given to Jupiter, with which to rout
> Armies of men. With this in hand he led
> The assailants on."

BRYANT, *Iliad*, Book XV.

Against an attack so led the bravery of the Greeks was of little avail. Numbers of their warriors were slain, and the rest fled back to their camp, pursued by Hector and his triumphant hosts. This time the Trojans were not hindered by the trench or the wall, for Apollo with his mighty feet trampled down the earth banks, and overthrew the great wall as easily as a child at play on the beach overthrows a tiny mound of sand.

Then a fierce struggle took place, the Greeks fighting with desperate fury to defend their ships, which the Trojans, with lighted torches in their hands, tried to set on fire. At one of the galleys there was a terrific conflict. Hector, having grasped the vessel by the stern, called to his men to bring on their flaming brands, while the mighty Ajax stood on the rowers' bench, ready with his long spear to strike the assailants back.

On the blade of that long spear
The hero took them as they came, and slew
In close encounter twelve before the fleet.

BRYANT, *Iliad*, Book XV.

But at last the brave son of Telamon was forced to give way, Hector having cut his spear shaft in two by a stroke of his huge sword. Then the Trojans hurled forward their blazing torches, and the ship was soon wrapped in flames. The Greeks were now in the greatest peril. No hope seemed left to them to save their fleet from destruction. But help came from an unexpected quarter. Patroclus, the friend and companion of Achilles, had been watching the terrible conflict at the ships. As soon as he saw the vessel on fire he hurried to the tent of the Myrmidonian chief, and with tears in his eyes implored him to have pity on his perishing countrymen.

"The Greeks," said he, "are sorely pressed. Their bravest leaders are wounded, while you sit here, giving way to your wrath. If you will not yourself go to their rescue, at least permit me to lead the Myrmidons to battle, and let me wear your armor. The Trojans at the sight of it may think I am Achilles, and be so terrified that our people may have a little breathing time."

To this proposal Achilles assented, but he warned Patroclus not to pursue the Trojans too far, lest he might meet his death at the hands of one of the gods. "Rescue our good ships," said he, "but when you have driven the enemy from the fleet, return hither."

With joy and eager haste Patroclus put on the armor of Achilles. Then the great chief himself marshaled his Myrmidons in battle array, after which he addressed them, bidding them fight valiantly. The occasion, he said, had now come which they had so long desired, for they had often blamed him because he had kept them from joining their countrymen in the field. Fierce and fearless these Myrmidons were, and over two thousand strong.

> Achilles, dear to Jupiter, had led
> Fifty swift barks to Ilium, and in each
> Were fifty men, companions at the oar.

BRYANT, *Iliad*, Book XVI.

Patroclus now mounted the chariot of Achilles, with the brave Au-tom'e-don as charioteer, a hero next in valor to the renowned son of Peleus himself. There were three horses in the team, Xanthus and Ba'li-us, both of immortal breed, and fleet as the wind, and Ped'a-sus, which, though of mortal stock, was a match for the others in speed.

> Like in strength, in swiftness and in grace,
> A mortal courser match'd the immortal race.

POPE, *Iliad*, Book XVI.

Great was the terror of the Trojans when they beheld the Myrmidons march forth to battle.

> Every heart grew faint
> With fear; the close ranks wavered; for they thought
> That the swift son of Peleus at the fleet
> Had laid aside his wrath, and was again
> The friend of Agamemnon. Eagerly
> They looked around for an escape from death.

BRYANT, *Iliad*, Book XVI.

The Greek fleet was soon out of danger, for Patroclus and his Myrmidons, having furiously attacked the Trojans, quickly

Michael Clarke

drove them away from the burning vessel and put out the fire. Having thus saved the ships, the Myrmidonian warriors, aided by the other Greeks, then drove the Trojans with great slaughter from the camp into the plain, and on towards the walls of the city.

> In that scattered conflict of the chiefs
> Each Argive slew a warrior.

BRYANT, *Iliad*, Book XVI.

Even the mighty Hector was not able to stop the flight of the panic-stricken Trojans, who seemed for the moment to have lost all their courage, so great was their fear at the name of Achilles. The hero Sarpedon at the head of his brave Lycians attempted to turn back the onset of the Myrmidons, and he sought out their leader to engage him in single combat. Both warriors sprang from their chariots at the same moment, and rushed at each other, hurling their spears. Twice Sarpedon missed his foe, but one of the weapons killed Pedasus, the horse of "mortal stock." The leader of the Myrmidons cast his javelin with truer aim, for it pierced the Lycian chief right in the breast, and the hero fell like a tall pine tree falling in the forest at the last blow of the woodman's ax.

Then a fierce conflict took place over the body, the Greeks seeking to obtain possession of the warrior's armor, which they did after many on both sides had been slain in the struggle. The body itself was sent by Apollo, at Jupiter's command, to Lycia, that the hero's kinsmen there might perform funeral rites in his honor.

> In robes of heaven
> He clothed him, giving him to Sleep and Death,
> Twin brothers, and swift bearers of the dead,
> And they, with speed conveying it, laid down
> The corpse in Lycia's broad and opulent realm.

Jupiter thus honored Sarpedon because the hero was his own son. He would have saved him from the spear of Patroclus, but the Fates had decreed that Sarpedon should die in the battle, and the decrees of the Fates were not to be set aside even by Jove himself.

Patroclus, too, was doomed to fall in the conflict of the day, and the moment was now at hand. Forgetting the warning Achilles had given him, he pursued the Trojans up to the very gates of the city. Then he attempted to scale the wall, but he was driven back by Apollo, who spoke to him in threatening voice, saying that not by him should Troy be taken, nor by his chief, though mightier far than he. Hastily Patroclus withdrew from the walls, fearing the wrath of the archer god, but he continued to deal death among the Trojans as they came within reach of his weapons.

At last Hector, urged by Apollo, rushed forward in his chariot to encounter Patroclus. The Myrmidon leader lifted a large stone, and flung it with all his force at the Trojan chief as he approached. It missed Hector, but killed Ce-bri'o-nes, his charioteer, and while they fought over the body, each helped by brave comrades, many more on both sides were laid in the dust. Again the archer god interfered, this time coming unseen behind Patroclus, and striking him with his open palm between the shoulders. The hero staggered under the blow, his huge spear was shattered in his hands, and his shield dropped to the ground. Then Eu-phor'bus, a Dardanian chief, hurried forward, and with his lance wounded him in the back. Thus disarmed and almost overpowered, Patroclus turned to seek refuge in the ranks of his friends. As he was retreating, Hector rushed upon him, and thrusting a spear deep into his body, gave the brave warrior his death wound.

The hero fell
With clashing mail, and all the Greeks beheld
His fall with grief.

BRYANT, *Iliad*, Book XVI.

Then there was a long and terrific fight around the corpse of the fallen champion. The description of it occupies a whole book of the Iliad. The armor Patroclus wore was, as we have seen, the rich armor of Achilles, and the Trojans were eager to get possession of it. They wished also to get possession of the hero's body, that his friends might not have the satisfaction of performing the usual funeral rites in his honor. Menelaus was the first to stand guard over the body, and Euphorbus was the first to fall in the fight. Hector had gone in pursuit of the charioteer, Automedon, thinking to slay him, and capture the immortal horses of Achilles. But Apollo warned him against the attempt.

"Hector, thou art pursuing what thy feet
Will never overtake, the steeds which draw
The chariot of Achilles. Hard it were
For mortal man to tame them or to guide,
Save for Achilles, goddess-born. Meanwhile
Hath warlike Menelaus, Atreus' son,
Guarding the slain Patroclus, overthrown
Euphorbus, bravest of the Trojan host."

BRYANT, *Iliad*, Book XVII.

Hearing these words Hector hastened back to where the corpse of the Greek hero was lying. When Menelaus saw him approaching, he withdrew, and hurried off to seek help, for he feared to encounter the terrible Trojan leader. Then Hector stripped Patroclus of the splendid armor of Achilles, and he was about dragging away the body, but just at that moment Ajax rushed up. Hector now retreated, leaping into his chariot and giving the glittering armor to his friends to be carried away to Troy.

For thus fleeing from the fight the Trojan chief was severely rebuked by Glau'cus, a Lycian warrior, who had been the comrade of the brave Sarpedon. Glaucus wished to get the body of Patroclus so that with it he might ransom Sarpedon's armor from the Greeks. Hector answered Glaucus, saying that he feared not the battle's fury, as he would presently show. Then he put on the armor of Achilles and he called to the Trojans to follow him, promising a rich reward to the warrior who should carry off the body for which they were going to fight.

> "To him who from the field will drag and bring
> The slain Patroclus to the Trojan knights,
> Compelling Ajax to give way,—to him
> I yield up half the spoil; the other half
> I keep, and let his glory equal mine."

BRYANT, *Iliad*, Book XVII.

With Hector at their head the Trojans now rushed forward. Ajax, seeing them advance, bade Menelaus summon the other Greek warriors to help in defending the body of their countryman. Quickly they were called and quickly they came. Then hand to hand and sword to sword both armies fought, and the battle raged furiously round the corpse of Patroclus.

> They of Ilium strove
> To drag it to the city, they of Greece,
> To bear it to the fleet.

BRYANT, *Iliad*, Book XVII.

At last Menelaus and a brother warrior lifted up the body and bore it away towards the trench. The Trojans followed, but the two Ajaxes turned around and, facing the pursuers, fought with heroic bravery to hold them back.

> Thus, in hot pursuit
> And close array, the Trojans following strook
> With swords and two-edged spears;
> but when the twain
> Turned and stood firm to meet them, every cheek
> Grew pale, and not a single Trojan dared
> Draw near the Greeks to combat for the corse.
> Thus rapidly they bore away the dead
> Toward their good galleys from the battlefield.
> Onward with them the furious battle swept.

BRYANT, *Iliad*, Book XVII.

Meanwhile Antilochus, the son of Nestor, was sent from the field to carry to Achilles the sad news of the death of Patroclus. The chief was just then sitting near his ships thinking over the event which he feared had already happened, for the shouts of the Greeks as they fled from the plain pursued by the Trojans, had reached his ears. Upon learning the tidings brought by Antilochus, the hero burst into a fit of grief, tearing his hair, throwing himself on the earth, and uttering loud lamentations. His goddess mother, Thetis, in her father's palace beneath the waves, heard his cries. She hastened up, attended by a number of sea nymphs, and, embracing her son, inquired the cause of his grief. Achilles told her of the death of his dear friend, and then said:

> "No wish
> Have I to live or to concern myself
> In men's affairs, save this: that Hector first,
> Pierced by my spear, shall yield his life, and pay
> The debt of vengeance for Patroclus slain."

BRYANT, *Iliad*, Book XVIII.

The weeping mother, wishing to save her son, told him of the fate which had decreed that his own death should soon follow that of Hector.

"Ah then, I see thee dying, see thee dead!
When Hector falls, thou diest."

POPE, *Iliad*, Book XVIII.

But the warning of Thetis was in vain. "Let my death come," said he, "when the gods will it. I shall have revenge on Hector, by whose hand my friend has been slain."

Seeing that she could not induce him to alter his purpose, his mother reminded him that his bright armor had been seized by the Trojans. She bade him therefore not go to battle until she should bring him new armor made by Vulcan, which she promised to do early next morning. Then she commanded the other nymphs to return to their ocean home, and she herself ascended to Olympus, to ask the god of smiths to forge glittering armor for her son.

Meantime the fight over the body of Patroclus still continued. The Greeks were now driven to their ships, and in danger of being totally defeated. Three times Hector seized the body by the feet, to drag it away, and three times the mighty Ajaxes forced him back. Still again he seized it, and this time he would have borne it away, had not Juno sent Iris down to Achilles to bid him hasten to the relief of his friends.

"But how," he asked, "can I go forth to the battle, since the enemy have my arms?" Iris answered:

Michael Clarke

"Go thou to the trench, and show thyself
To them of Troy, that, haply smit with fear,
They may desist from battle."

BRYANT, *Iliad*, Book XVIII.

Then the goddess Minerva spread a golden cloud around the head of Achilles, and she kindled in it a bright flame that streamed upward to the sky. And the hero went out beyond the wall, and stood beside the trench, and he shouted in a voice loud as a trumpet sound,—a shout that carried dismay into the ranks of the Trojans.

The hearts of all who heard that brazen voice
Were troubled, and their steeds with flowing manes
Turned backward with the chariots,—such the dread
Of coming slaughter
Thrice o'er the trench Achilles shouted; thrice
The men of Troy and their renowned allies
Fell into wild disorder. Then there died,
Entangled midst the chariots, and transfixed
By their own spears, twelve of their bravest chiefs.
The Greeks bore off Patroclus from the field
With eager haste, and placed him on a bier,
And there the friends that loved him gathered round
Lamenting.

BRYANT, *Iliad*, Book XVIII

So ended the long and terrible battle of the day, for Juno now commanded the sun to set. In obedience to the queen of heaven the god of light descended into the ocean streams, though unwillingly he did so, as it was earlier than the proper time for sunset.

The Trojan leaders, meanwhile, assembled in council on the plain to consider what preparations should be made for the battle of the morrow, in which, they knew, the terrible Achilles would take part. Po-lyd'a-mas, a prudent chief, proposed that they should withdraw into the city. There they might defend themselves from their ramparts, for even Achilles, with all his valor, would not be able to force his way through their strong walls. But Hector rejected this wise advice. He resolved to risk the chance of war in the open field, and let the god of battles decide who should win.

"Soon as the morn the purple orient warms,
Fierce on yon navy will we pour our arms.
If great Achilles rise in all his might,
His be the danger: I shall stand the fight.
Honor, ye gods! or let me gain or give;
And live he glorious, whosoe'er shall live!"

POPE, *Iliad*, Book XVIII.

XI. END OF THE WRATH OF ACHILLES
—DEATH OF HECTOR

Thetis faithfully performed her promise to Achilles. Having ascended to the top of Olympus, she found the god of smiths busy in his forge, a workshop so magnificent that it was a wonder to the gods themselves.

> Silver-footed Thetis came
> Meanwhile to Vulcan's halls, eternal, gemmed
> With stars, a wonder to the immortals, wrought
> Of brass by the lame god. She found him there
> Sweating and toiling, and with busy hand
> Plying the bellows.

BRYANT, *Iliad*, Book XVIII.

Vulcan willingly consented to make the armor as Thetis requested, for she had been his friend and had protected him in his infancy, when his mother Juno threw him out of heaven into the sea. Juno did this because Vulcan was not a good-looking child. He was, in fact, so ugly that his mother could not bear the sight of him, and so she cast him out of Olympus. But Thetis and her sister Eu-ryn'o-me received him in their arms as he fell, and for nine years they nursed and took care of him in their father's palace beneath the waves. Gladly, therefore, Vulcan set to work at the request of his old friend. In his workshop were immense furnaces, and he had plenty of precious material in store.

> Upon the fire
> He laid impenetrable brass, and tin,
> And precious gold and silver; on its block
> Placed the huge anvil, took the ponderous sledge,
> And held the pincers in the other hand.

BRYANT, *Iliad*, Book XVIII.

And first he made a shield, large and massive, upon which he wrought figures of the earth and the sky, the sun, moon, and stars, with many other beautiful designs. He wrought upon it numerous scenes of human life,—representations of war and peace, of battles and sieges, of reapers in the harvest fields, of shepherds tending their flocks, of vintagers gathering their grapes; and scenes of festivity with music, song, and dancing. Homer gives a long and splendid description of this wonderful shield. When Vulcan had finished it, he forged a corselet brighter than fire, and greaves of tin, and a helmet with crest of gold. Then he laid the magnificent armor at the feet of Thetis, and the goddess bore it away and carried it down to the Grecian camp in the early morning to present it to her son.

> Like a falcon in her flight,
> Down plunging from Olympus capped with snow,
> She bore the shining armor Vulcan gave.

BRYANT, *Iliad*, Book XVIII.

Great was the delight of Achilles on seeing the beautiful armor and the marvelous workmanship of its various parts. And now he hastened to prepare for battle. First he went along the beach from tent to tent, calling with a mighty shout on his brother chiefs to assemble. When all were together he spoke friendly words to Agamemnon, expressing sorrow that

Michael Clarke

strife had come between them, and declaring that his wrath was now ended.

> "Here then my anger ends; let war succeed,
> And even as Greece has bled, let Ilion bleed.
> Now call the hosts, and try if in our sight
> Troy yet shall dare to camp a second night!"

POPE, *Iliad*, Book XIX.

Agamemnon, too, spoke words of peace and friendship, and all the chiefs rejoiced that the anger of Achilles, which had brought so many woes upon the Greeks, was at length appeased. Then the troops took their morning meal, and when they had refreshed themselves with food and drink, they marched forth to the field. Achilles, having put on his bright armor, mounted his chariot, to which were yoked the two immortal and swift-footed steeds, Xanthus and Balius.

And here a wonderful thing occurred. When the hero spoke to the animals, charging them in loud and terrible voice to bring him back safely from the battle, and not leave him dead on the plain, as they had left Patroclus, Xanthus, to whom Juno had, for the moment, given the power of speech, replied to the words of his master, saying that it was not through any fault of himself and his comrade that Patroclus had been slain, but by the interference of Apollo. He also warned Achilles that the hour of his own death was near at hand.

> "Not through our crime, or slowness in the course,
> Fell thy Patroclus, but by heavenly force;   .
> The bright far-shooting god who gilds the day
> (Confess'd we saw him) tore his arms away.
> No—could our swiftness o'er the winds prevail,
> Or beat the pinions of the western gale,
> All were in vain—the Fates thy death demand,

Due to a mortal and immortal hand."

POPE, *Iliad*, Book XIX.

But Achilles already knew his fate, and he was prepared to meet it with courage.

"I know my fate: to die, to see no more
My much-loved parents, and my native shore—
Enough—when heaven ordains, I sink in night:
Now perish Troy!" He said, and rush'd to fight.

POPE, *Iliad*, Book XIX,

In the battle which now began many of the gods took active part, Jupiter, at a council on Mount Olympus, having given them permission to do so. Down to the plain before Troy they sped with haste, Juno, Minerva, Neptune, Mercury, and Vulcan taking the side of the Greeks, and Mars, Apollo, Venus, Diana, Latona, and the river god, Xanthus, going to the assistance of the Trojans.

Meantime Achilles, having rushed forth to the field, plunged into the thick of the fight, eagerly seeking for Hector. But first he met Æneas, whom Apollo had urged to encounter him. Achilles warned the Trojan hero to withdraw from the battle.

"Once already," said he, "I forced you to flee before my spear, running fast down Ida's slopes. I counsel you now to retire, lest evil happen to you."

Æneas answered that he was not to be thus frightened, as if he were a beardless boy. "I am the son of the goddess Venus," said he, "and my father, Anchises, was descended from Jove himself. We are not here, however, to talk, but to fight, and words will not turn me from my purpose."

So saying, Æneas hurled his spear. It struck the shield of Achilles with a ringing sound, and passed through two of its folds.

Vulcan's skill
Fenced with five folds the disk,—the outer two
Of brass, the inner two of tin; between
Was one of gold, and there the brazen spear   Was stayed.

BRYANT, *Iliad*, Book XX.

Achilles now cast his heavy javelin. Through the shield of Æneas it crashed, but, as the hero stooped to avoid it, the spear passed over his shoulder, and plunged deep into the earth. Then with sword in hand, the Myrmidonian chief rushed furiously upon Æneas. He would probably have slain him, had not Neptune interfered. But the ocean god spread a mist over the eyes of the Greek warrior, and carried Æneas away in safety to the rear of the battlefield. The Trojan prince was thus preserved because the Dardan race, to which he belonged, was beloved by Jupiter. Moreover it was decreed by the Fates that the son of Anchises should, in later times, rule over a Trojan people, and that his sons' sons should rule after him.

Having placed Æneas out of danger, Neptune removed the mist from the eyes of Achilles. The hero, on looking about him, was amazed at not seeing the foe with whom, only an instant before, he had been in fierce conflict. But he did not wait to think over this strange occurrence. Rushing into the midst of the Trojans, he smote down warrior after warrior, as they came within reach of his spear. Amongst them was Pol-y-do'rus, the youngest son of Priam. His father had forbidden him to go into the battle, because he loved him most of all his sons. But Polydorus was a brave youth, and he wished to show his swiftness, for in speed of foot he excelled all the young men of Troy.

He ranged the field, until he lost his life.
Him with a javelin the swift-footed son
Of Peleus smote as he was hurrying by.

BRYANT, *Iliad*, Book XX.

Now Hector had been warned by Apollo to avoid meeting
Achilles, but when he saw his young brother slain, he could
no longer stand aloof. He therefore sprang forward to attack
the son of Thetis. As soon as Achilles saw the Trojan chief,
he bounded towards him, crying out:

"Draw nearer that thou mayst the sooner die."

BRYANT, *Iliad*, Book XX.

Hector replied in words of defiance, and then brandished and
hurled forth his spear. But Minerva turned it aside, and it
missed its aim. Then Achilles, with a wild shout, rushed
against his enemy. Apollo now came to the rescue, covering
the Trojan hero in a veil of clouds, and taking him away
from the conflict. The enraged Achilles struck into the dense
mist with his sword again and again, and in loud voice
reproached Hector for what seemed to be his cowardly flight.

"Hound as thou art, thou hast once more escaped
Thy death; for it was near. Again the hand
Of Phœbus rescues thee. I shall meet thee yet
And end thee utterly, if any god
Favor me also. I will now pursue
And strike the other Trojan warriors down."

BRYANT, *Iliad*, Book XX.

The enraged hero then attacked the Trojans so furiously that
they fled before him in dismay. Some rushed towards the
gates of the city, others to the Xanthus, into which they

leaped in such numbers that the river was soon filled with a crowd of steeds and men.

So, plunged in Xanthus by Achilles' force,
Roars the resounding surge with men and horse.

POPE, *Iliad*, Book XXI.

But now the terrible Myrmidonian chief descended from his chariot, and with sword in hand pursued the Trojans into the water. There he slew so many that the stream became blocked with the bodies of the dead. The river god, roused to anger, called to Achilles in a loud voice from the depths of the Xanthus, saying that if he meant to destroy the whole Trojan race, he must do it on the plain, and not stop the waters in their course to the sea.

"For now my pleasant waters, in their flow,
Are choked with heaps of dead, and I no more
Can pour them into the great deep, so thick
The corpses clog my bed, while thou dost slay
And sparest not."

BRYANT, *Iliad*, Book XXI.

Achilles answered that he would not cease to slay the treaty-breaking Trojans until they were punished as they deserved. At this the river god was so enraged that he sent his waters with tremendous force against the hero. The waves now surged around Achilles, beating upon his shield, and buffeting him so violently that he was in danger of being overwhelmed. He saved himself only by grasping the bough of an elm tree which grew on the river's edge, and so gaining the bank. Then the angry god, rising in greater fury, swept his mighty billows out upon the plain. The Greek hero bravely attempted to fight this new enemy, but his valor and his weapons were powerless against such an attack.

As often as the noble son
Of Peleus made a stand in hope to know
Whether the deathless gods of the great heaven
Conspired to make him flee, so often came
A mighty billow of the Jove-born stream
And drenched his shoulders. Then again he sprang
Away; the rapid torrent made his knees
To tremble, while it swept, where'er he trod,
The earth from underneath his feet.

BRYANT, *Iliad*, Book XXI.

Achilles now prayed to the gods for help, and Neptune and Minerva came and encouraged him, saying that he was not to be thus conquered. Still as Xanthus called upon his brother river, Simois, to join him in defense of King Priam's noble city, it might have fared badly with the Greeks, had not Vulcan come to their help. At the request of Juno the god of fire sent down a vast quantity of flames, which scorched and dried up the plain, and burned the trees and reeds on the banks of the rivers. Vulcan began to dry up even the rivers themselves. Then Xanthus became terrified and begged for mercy, promising that he would not again interfere in the fight on either side.

"Oh Vulcan! oh! what power resists thy might?
I faint, I sink, unequal to the fight—
I yield—Let Ilion fall; if fate decree—
Ah—bend no more thy fiery arms on me!"

POPE, *Iliad*, Book XXI.

It was not, however, until Juno entreated him to do so, that Vulcan withdrew his flames, and the rivers were permitted to flow on again in peace and safety. Achilles now renewed his attack on the Trojans. The gods also rushed into the conflict. Mars launched his brazen spear at Minerva, but, with the

Michael Clarke

terrible ægis, the goddess warded off the blow. Then Minerva lifted up a great rough stone and hurled it at Mars, striking him on the neck, and stretching him senseless on the ground.

> He fell
> With nerveless limbs, and covered, as he lay,
> Seven acres of the field.

BRYANT, *Iliad*, Book XXI.

Venus hastened to the relief of the wounded god, and, taking him by the hand, led him away groaning with pain. Juno, who had been a spectator of the fight, now approached Minerva, and urged her to attack Venus. She gladly consented to do as the queen of heaven desired. Following up the goddess of beauty, Minerva gave her a mighty blow on the breast, throwing her prostrate on the earth. At the same time Neptune challenged Apollo to fight. He reminded him, too, of King Laomedon's conduct toward both of them, many years before, and reproached him for being now on the side of the descendants of that faithless king. But Apollo refused to fight with the ocean god.

> "Thou wouldst not deem me wise, should I contend
> With thee, O Neptune, for the sake of men,
> Who flourish like the forest leaves awhile,
> And feed upon the fruits of earth and then
> Decay and perish."

BRYANT, *Iliad*, Book XXI.

But though Apollo would not fight with Neptune, he continued to help the Trojans. Achilles had driven them in terror up under their walls, and King Priam had ordered the gates to be thrown open to admit the flying hosts. Multitudes of them rushed in, while the furious son of Thetis pressed on behind. It was a moment of danger for Troy, and the Greeks might soon have taken the city, if Apollo had not encouraged young Agenor, the son of Antenor, to attack Achilles. The brave youth advanced, and cast his spear, striking the hero at the knee. But it could not pierce the armor Vulcan had made. Then the Greek chief aimed at Agenor, and again Apollo came to the rescue, concealing the Trojan youth in a veil of darkness, and carrying him safely away. But in an instant the god returned, and, taking upon himself Agenor's shape and appearance, stood for a moment in front of Achilles. Then he turned and fled along the plain, followed fast by the enraged Greek. Thus Apollo gave the Trojans time to get within the city and shut their gates.

> Achilles chased the god
> Ever before him, yet still near, across
> The fruitful fields, to the deep-eddied stream
> Of Xanthus; for Apollo artfully
> Made it to seem that he should soon o'ertake
> His flying foe, and thus beguiled him on.
> Meanwhile the routed Trojans gladly thronged
> Into the city, filled the streets, and closed
> The portals.

BRYANT, *Iliad*, Book XXI.

Hector alone of all the Trojans remained outside the walls, standing in front of the Scæan Gate. Achilles still pursued Apollo, thinking that he was Agenor, but at last the god made himself known to his pursuer. The hero reproached him angrily for his deception, and then with the utmost speed he hastened across the plain towards the city. From the ramparts the aged King Priam beheld him coming, and in piteous words he cried out to Hector, imploring him to take refuge within the walls. Queen Hecuba, too, with tears in her eyes, begged her son to withdraw, and not be so mad as to encounter the terrible Greek chief alone. But Hector would not yield to the entreaties of his weeping parents. He had refused to take the advice of Polydamas to withdraw into the city on the previous night, and if he should pass within the walls now, after Achilles had slain so many of the Trojans, Polydamas would be the first to reproach him. Thus the hero reasoned with himself and so he resolved to stand and face his foe.

> "No—if I e'er return, return I must
> Glorious, my country's terror laid in dust:
> Or if I perish, let her see me fall
> In field at least, and fighting for her wall."

POPE, *Iliad*, Book XXII.

Achilles now approached. Terrible he was in appearance. His great javelin quivered fearfully on his shoulder, and a light as of blazing fire, or of the rising sun, shone from his heavenly armor. Hector trembled with fear when he looked upon the Grecian leader. So great was his terror that he did not dare to wait, but fled away round the city wall. Achilles quickly pursued him, as a hawk pursues a dove. They ran till they came to two springs where the stream of the Xanthus rose. From one of these springs a hot vapor ascended, like smoke from fire, and from the other a current cold as ice issued even in summer. Past these the warriors swept on.

> One fled, and one pursued,—
> A brave man fled, a braver followed close,
> And swiftly both. Not for a common prize,
> A victim from the herd, a bullock's hide,
> Such as reward the fleet of foot, they ran,—
> The race was for the knightly Hector's life.

BRYANT, *Iliad*, Book XXII.

Three times they ran round the walls, in sight of the Greeks and Trojans. The gods of heaven, too, were looking on from the top of Mount Olympus, and Jupiter, taking pity on Hector, thought that they should save him from death. But Minerva protested. His doom, she said, had been fixed by the Fates, and even Jupiter could not alter it—at least not with the approval of the other gods. The cloud-compelling king was obliged to give way, and so the Trojan chief was left to his fate. Then Minerva rushed down to the field, and still Hector fled and Achilles pursued. As often as they passed around, Hector attempted to approach the gates, hoping for help from his friends. But each time Achilles got before him and turned him away towards the plain; and he made a sign to the Greeks that none of them should cast a spear, for he wished that he alone should have all the glory of slaying the greatest of the Trojan heroes.

Now Apollo had been helping Hector, giving him strength and speed, but when, for the fourth time, the heroes reached the Xanthus springs, Jupiter raised high the golden balance of fate. There were two lots in the scales, one for the son of Peleus, the other for the Trojan chief. By the middle the king of heaven held the balance, and the lot of Hector sank down. Immediately Apollo departed from the field, for he could no longer go against the Fates. Then Minerva came close to Hector's side, and, taking the form and voice of his brother Deiphobus, she urged him to stand and fight Achilles.

"Hard pressed I find thee, brother, by the swift
Achilles, who, with feet that never rest,
Pursues thee round the walls of Priam's town.
But let us make a stand and beat him back."

BRYANT, *Iliad*, Book XXII.

Thus encouraged, as he thought by his brother, whom he was surprised to see at his side, for he believed him to be in the

Michael Clarke

city, the Trojan hero turned around, and was soon face to face with his great foe. Knowing that the hour had now come when one of them must die, Hector proposed to Achilles that they should make a covenant, or agreement, between them that the victor in the fight should give the other's body to his friends, so that funeral rites might be performed. But the wrathful Achilles refused. He would have no covenant with his enemy.

"Accursed Hector, never talk to me
Of covenants. Men and lions plight no faith,
Nor wolves agree with lambs, but each must plan
Evil against the other. So between
Thyself and me no compact can exist,
Or understood intent. First, one of us
Must fall and yield his life blood to the god   Of battles."

BRYANT, *Iliad*, Book XXII.

Then the fight began, Achilles first cast his spear. It was a weapon heavy, huge, and strong, that no mortal arm but his own could wield. Its shaft was made of a tree which the famous Chi'ron, instructor of heroes in the art of war, had cut on Mount Pe'li-on and given to the father of Achilles.

His strength
Alone sufficed to wield it. 'Twas an ash
Which Chiron felled in Pelion's top, and gave
To Peleus, that it yet might be the death   Of heroes.

BRYANT, *Iliad*, Book XVI.

The Trojan chief stooped to avoid the blow, and the spear, passing over him, sunk in the earth. Minerva, unseen by Hector, plucked it out and gave it back to Achilles. Hector now launched his weapon. With true aim he hurled it, for it struck the center of his antagonist's shield, but the workmanship of Vulcan was not to be pierced, and so the javelin of the Trojan hero bounded from the brazen armor and fell to the ground. He called loudly to Deiphobus for another spear. There was no answer, and then looking around him he discovered that he had been deceived.

> All comfortless he stands; then, with a sigh:
> "'Tis so—Heaven wills it, and my hour is nigh.
> I deem'd Deiphobus had heard my call,
> But he secure lies guarded in the wall.
> A god deceived me; Pallas, 'twas thy deed,
> Death and black fate approach! 'tis I must bleed."

POPE, *Iliad*, Book XXII.

Nevertheless, Hector resolved to fight bravely to the end, and so he drew his sword and rushed upon Achilles. The Greek warrior, watching his foe closely as he approached, noticed an opening in his armor, where the collar of the corselet joined the shoulder. At that spot he furiously thrust his speat, and pierced the Trojan hero through the neck. Hector fell to the ground, mortally wounded. In his dying moments he begged Achilles to send his body to his parents, telling him that they would give large ransom in gold. But his entreaties were in vain. Neither by prayers nor by promise of gold could the conqueror be moved. The last words of Hector were words warning Achilles of his own doom:

> "A day will come when fate's decree
> And angry gods shall wreak this wrong on thee;
> Phœbus and Paris shall avenge my fate,
> And stretch thee here before the Scæan Gate."
> He ceased. The Fates suppress'd his laboring breath,
> And his eyes stiffen'd at the hand of death.

POPE, *Iliad*, Book XXII.

So died the great champion of the Trojans. The Greeks crowded around the dead hero, admiring his stature and beautiful figure, and remarking one to another that Hector was far less dangerous to touch now than when he was setting fire to their fleet.

But the anger of Achilles was not appeased even by the death of his foe. Eager for still more vengeance, he bound the feet of the dead hero with leather thongs to the back of his chariot, leaving the head to trail along the ground, and thus he drove to the ships, dragging the noble Hector in the dust.

The Trojans, beholding this dreadful spectacle from the walls of the city, broke out into loud lamentations, and King Priam and Queen Hecuba were almost distracted with grief. Andromache had not been a witness of the combat. She was at home with her maids, making preparations for Hector's return from the battle, and was therefore unaware of the terrible events which had taken place. But the sound of the wailing on the ramparts having reached her ears, she rushed forth from the palace, fearful that some evil had happened to her husband. Hastening through the streets to the Scæan Gate, she ascended the tower, and looking out on the plain, saw the body of her beloved Hector dragged behind the wheels of the chariot of Achilles. Overpowered with grief at the sight, the unhappy woman sank fainting into the arms of her attendants.

> A sudden darkness shades her swimming eyes:
> She faints, she falls; her breath, her color flies.
> Her hair's fair ornaments, the braids that bound,
> The net that held them, and the wreath that crown'd,
> The veil and diadem flew far away
> (The gift of Venus on her bridal day).
> Around a train of weeping sisters stands
> To raise her sinking with assistant hands.

POPE, *Iliad*, Book XXII.

While the Trojans thus mourned the loss of their chief, his body was dragged into the Grecian camp and flung on the beach beside the ships. Preparations were then made for funeral services in honor of Patroclus. The ceremonies occupied three days. A vast quantity of wood was cut down on Mount Ida, and carried to the plain, where the logs were heaped together in an immense pile, a hundred feet square. Upon this they placed the corpse. They next put upon the pile the fat of several oxen, that it might the more easily burn, and they slew and laid upon it the dead man's horses. Achilles cut off a lock of his own hair and put it in the dead hero's hand, and each of the other warriors placed a lock of his hair on the body.

Torches were now applied, and they prayed to the wind gods, Bo're-as and Zeph'y-rus, to send strong breezes to fan the flames. All through the night the pile blazed with a mighty roar, and in the morning, when it was consumed, the embers were quenched with wine, and the bones of Patroclus were gathered up and inclosed in a golden urn. On the spot where the pyre had stood they raised a mound of earth as a monument to the hero.

Then there were funeral games at which valuable prizes, given by Achilles, were competed for,—prizes of gold and silver, and shining weapons, and vases, and steeds, and oxen. Diomede won the prize in the chariot race, for he ran with the immortal horses he had taken in battle from Æneas. In the wrestling match Ulysses and Ajax Telamon were the rival champions. Both displayed such strength and skill that it could not be decided which was the victor, and so a prize of equal value was given to each. Ajax Telamon also competed with Diomede in a combat with swords, and both were declared equal and received each a prize.

Michael Clarke

In the contest with bow and arrows, Teu'cer and Me-ri'o-nes were the competitors, and a dove tied to the top of a mast fixed in the ground, was the object aimed at. Teucer missed the bird, but he struck and cut the cord that fastened her to the pole, and she flew up into the heavens. Then Meriones shot at her with his arrow. The weapon pierced the dove beneath the wing and she fell to the earth. This feat was greatly admired by the spectators, and Meriones received as his prize ten double-bladed battle-axes. To Teucer, whose performance was also much applauded, a prize of ten single-bladed axes was given.

Thus did Achilles honor his dead friend by funeral rites and funeral games. But his wrath against Hector still continued, even when he had dragged the hero's body at his chariot wheels three times round the tomb of Patroclus. This cruel insult he repeated at dawn for several days. But Apollo watched the body.

> Apollo, moved
> With pity for the hero, kept him free
> From soil or stain, though dead, and o'er him held
> The golden ægis, lest, when roughly dragged
> Along the ground, the body might be torn.

> BRYANT, *Iliad*, Book XXIV.

But at last the gods, with the exception of Juno, were moved to pity, and on the twelfth day from the death of the Trojan hero, Jupiter summoned Thetis to Olympus, and bade her command Achilles to restore Hector's body to his parents. He also sent Iris with a message to King Priam, telling him to go to the Greek fleet, bearing with him a suitable ransom for his son. Thetis promptly carried out the order of Jupiter. She told her son of the command of the king of heaven, and Achilles answered that since it was the will of Jove he was ready to obey.

"Let him who brings the ransom come and take
The body, if it be the will of Jove."

BRYANT, *Iliad*, Book XXIV.

Joyfully the aged Priam received the message of Iris, and he made haste to set out for the Grecian camp. He took with him costly things as ransom,—ten talents of gold, and precious vases and goblets, and many beautiful robes of state. These were carried in a wagon drawn by four mules, which were driven by the herald Idæus. The king rode in his own chariot and he himself was the charioteer. As they crossed the plain they were met by the god Mercury, whom Jupiter had sent to conduct them safely to the tent of the Greek warrior.

"Haste, guide King Priam to the Grecian fleet,
Yet so that none may see him, and no Greek
Know of his coming, till he stand before   Pelides."

BRYANT, *Iliad*, Book XXIV.

Mercury mounted the chariot of Priam, and taking in his hands the reins, he drove rapidly towards the ships. When they came to the trenches the god cast the guards into a deep slumber, and so the Trojan king and his companion reached the tent of the chief of the Myrmidons, unseen by any of the Greeks. Then Mercury departed, and ascended to Olympus.

Achilles received his visitors respectfully, and the aged king, kissing the hero's hand, knelt down before him and begged him have pity on a father mourning for his son.

"For his sake I come
To the Greek fleet, and to redeem his corse
I bring uncounted ransom. O, revere
The gods, Achilles, and be merciful,

Michael Clarke

Calling to mind thy father! happier he
Than I; for I have borne what no man else
That dwells on earth could bear,—have laid my lips
Upon the hand of him who slew my son."

BRYANT, *Iliad*, Book XXIV.

The Greek chief, moved by this appeal, replied in kind words and accepted the ransom, after which he caused Priam and Idæus to sit down and refresh themselves with food and drink, and invited them to remain with him for the night. He also granted a truce of twelve days for funeral rites in honor of Hector.

Early in the morning the Trojan king and his herald arose, and Mercury again descended from Olympus to conduct them safely from the Grecian camp. Quickly they yoked their steeds, and mournfully they drove across the plain to the city. Cassandra, who stood watching on the citadel of Pergamus, saw them coming, and she cried out in a loud voice to the people, bidding them go and meet their dead hero.

"If e'er ye rush'd in crowds, with vast delight,
To hail your hero glorious from the fight,
Now meet him dead, and let your sorrows flow;
Your common triumph, and your common woe."

POPE, *Iliad*, Book XXIV.

Amid the lamentations of the people the corpse was borne through the streets to the royal palace, where it was placed on a magnificent couch. Then Andromache and Queen Hecuba approached the body and wept aloud, each in turn uttering words of grief. Helen, too, came to mourn over Hector, and she spoke of his constant kindness and tenderness to her.

"O Hector, who wert dearest to my heart
Of all my husband's brothers,—for the wife
Am I of godlike Paris, him whose fleet
Brought me to Troy,—would I had sooner died!
And now the twentieth year is past since first
I came a stranger from my native shore,
Yet have I never heard from thee a word
Of anger or reproach. And when the sons
Of Priam, and his daughters, and the wives
Of Priam's sons, in all their fair array,
Taunted me grievously, or Hecuba
Herself,—for Priam ever was to me
A gracious father,—thou didst take my part
With kindly admonitions, and restrain
Their tongues with soft address and gentle words.
Therefore my heart is grieved, and I bewail
Thee and myself at once,—unhappy me!
For now I have no friend in all wide Troy,—
None to be kind to me: they hate me all."

BRYANT, *Iliad*, Book XXIV.

With the funeral of Hector the Iliad of Homer ends. The
poet's subject, as has been said, was the Wrath of Achilles,
and the poem properly closes when the results of the hero's
wrath have been related. The concluding lines of the twenty-
fourth, and last, book of the Iliad describe the funeral
ceremonies of Hector, which were the same as those
performed by the Greeks in honor of Patroclus.

Nine days they toiled
To bring the trunks of trees, and when the tenth
Arose to light the abodes of men, they brought
The corse of valiant Hector from the town
With many tears, and laid it on the wood
High up, and flung the fire to light the pile.

Michael Clarke

BRYANT, *Iliad*, Book XXIV.

The fire burned all night, and next day they gathered the
bones of Hector and placed them in a golden urn. Then they
buried the urn and erected a tomb over the grave.

> In haste they reared the tomb, with sentries set
> On every side, lest all too soon the Greeks
> Should come in armor to renew the war.
> When now the tomb was built, the multitude
> Returned, and in the halls where Priam dwelt,
> Nursling of Jove, were feasted royally.
> Such was the mighty Hector's burial rite.

BRYANT, *Iliad*, Book XXIV.

XII. DEATH OF ACHILLES
—FALL AND DESTRUCTION OF TROY

After the funeral of Hector the war was renewed. For a time
the Trojans remained within the walls of their city, which
were strong enough to resist all the assaults of the enemy.
But some allies having come to their assistance, they were
encouraged to sally forth again and fight the Greeks in the
open plain. The famous and beautiful Queen Pen-the-si-le'a
came with an army of her Am'a-zons, a nation of female
warriors who dwelt on the shores of the Black Sea.

> Penthesilea there with haughty grace,
> Leads to the wars an Amazonian race;
> In their right hands a pointed dart they wield;
> The left for ward, sustains the lunar shield.

VERGIL.

Brave as she was beautiful, the queen of the Amazons
scorned to remain behind the shelter of walls, and so, leading
her valiant band of women out through the gates, she made a
fierce attack on the Greeks. A terrific battle then began, and
many warriors on both sides were laid in the dust.
Penthesilea herself was slain by Achilles. The hero was
unwilling to fight with a woman, and he tried to avoid
meeting the queen, but she attacked him so furiously, first
hurling her spear, and then rushing upon him sword in hand,

that he was obliged to strike in self-defense. With a thrust of his lance he gave her a mortal wound, and the brave heroine fell, begging Achilles to permit her body to be taken away by her own people.

Filled with pity for the unfortunate queen, and with admiration for her courage and beauty, the hero granted the request. He even proposed that the Greeks should perform funeral rites and build a tomb in her honor. The foul-mouthed Thersites (mentioned in a previous chapter as having been chastised by Ulysses) scoffed at this proposal, and ridiculed Achilles, saying that he was not so soft-hearted in his treatment of Hector. Enraged at his insulting words, the chief of the Myrmidons struck him dead with a mighty blow of his fist.

Now Diomede was a relative of the unfortunate Thersites, and he demanded that Achilles should pay to the family of the dead man the fine required by Greek law for such offenses. Achilles refused, and he was about to retire again in anger from the war, and even to return home. But Ulysses persuaded Diomede to withdraw his claim, and so made peace between the two chiefs.

Another ally, and a very powerful one, now came to help the Trojans. This was Mem'non, king of Ethiopia, and nephew of Priam, being the son of Priam's brother Ti-tho'nus, and Au-ro'ra, goddess of the dawn. With an army of ten thousand men he arrived at Troy, and immediately entered the field to do battle with the Greeks. Again there was great slaughter of heroes on both sides. Memnon killed Antilochus, the son of Nestor, and Nestor challenged Memnon to single combat. But on account of the great age of the venerable Greek, the Ethiopian warrior declined to fight him. Achilles then challenged Memnon, and the two heroes fought in presence of both armies. The conflict was long and furious, for Memnon, too, had a suit of armor made for him by Vulcan, at the request of his goddess mother Aurora, and in strength and courage he was almost equal to Achilles. Once more, however, fortune favored the chief of the Myrmidons. The brave Memnon was slain, and Aurora bore away his body that funeral rites might be performed.

But the time was now at hand when the great warrior who so far had conquered in every fight was to meet his own doom. We have seen that Hector, as he lay dying in front of the Scæan Gate, warned Achilles that he himself should fall by the hand of Paris. This prophecy was fulfilled.

By the death of Memnon the Trojans were much discouraged. Their powerful allies had been defeated, and they were no longer able to hold the field against the enemy. Soon after the death of Memnon there was a great battle, in which the Greeks, headed by Achilles, drove them back to the city walls. Through the Scæan Gate, which lay open, the Trojans rushed in terror and confusion, the Greeks pressing on close behind. Achilles reached the gate, and was about to enter, when Paris aimed at him with an arrow. Guided by Apollo, the weapon struck the hero in the heel, the only part in which he could be fatally wounded.

The warrior fell to the ground, whereupon the Trojan prince hastened up and slew him with his sword. A terrific struggle took place over the body of the dead chief, but by mighty efforts Ajax Telamon and Ulysses succeeded in gaining possession of it, and carrying it to the Grecian camp. Deep was the grief of the Greeks at the death of their great champion. Magnificent funeral rites and games were celebrated in his honor, his goddess mother, Thetis, presiding over the ceremonies. After the body had been burned in the customary manner, the bones were placed in a vase of gold, made by Vulcan, and a vast mound was raised on the shore as a monument to the hero.

The sacred army of the warlike Greeks
Built up a tomb magnificently vast
Upon a cape of the broad Hellespont,
There to be seen, far off upon the deep,
By those who now are born, or shall be born
In future years.

BRYANT, *Odyssey*, Book XXIV.

The armor of Achilles was offered as a reward for the warrior who had fought most bravely in rescuing the body, and who had done most harm to the Trojans. To decide the question which of the Greek chiefs deserved this honor, it was resolved to take the votes of the Trojan prisoners then in the Greek camp, who had witnessed the struggle at the Scæan Gate. The majority of votes were in favor of Ulysses, and to him, therefore, the splendid shield and corselet and helmet and greaves, made by Vulcan for the son of Thetis, were given. Ajax was so disappointed and grieved at not having obtained the coveted prize that he became insane, and in his frenzy he slew himself with his own sword.

The Greeks had now lost their two most powerful warriors, and they began to think that it was impossible for them to take Troy by force, and that they must try other methods. So the wise Ulysses then set his brain to work to devise some stratagem by which the city might be taken. The first thing he did was to capture the Trojan prince and soothsayer, Helenus, who had gone out from the city to offer sacrifices in the temple of Apollo on Mount Ida. Calchas, the Greek soothsayer, had said that Helenus was the only mortal who knew by what means Troy could be conquered, and so Ulysses made him prisoner and threatened him with death if he did not tell.

Then Helenus told the Ithacan chief that before Troy could be taken three things must be done. First, he said, the Greeks must get the arrows of Hercules; next, they must carry away the sacred Palladium, for as long as it remained within the walls the city was safe; and, lastly, they must have the help of the son of Achilles.

Now the arrows of Hercules could be obtained only from Phil-oc-te'tes, a Greek chief who received them from Hercules himself. These arrows had been dipped in the blood of the hydra, a monster Hercules had slain. This made them poisonous, so that wounds inflicted by them were fatal. Philoctetes was with his countrymen at Aulis when they set sail for Troy, but he was bitten on the foot by a serpent, and the smell of the injured part being so offensive that his comrades could not endure it, he had been left behind, on the advice of Ulysses.

> Far in an island, suffering grievous pangs,—
> The hallowed isle of Lemnos. There the Greeks
> Left him, in torture from a venomed wound
> Made by a serpent's fangs. He lay and pined.

BRYANT, *Iliad*, Book II.

Ulysses now resolved to get Philoctetes to come to Troy, if he were still alive, and so, taking Diomede with him, he set out for Lemnos. They found him at the cave where they had left him ten years before. The wound was not yet healed, and he had suffered much, having had no means of existence except game which he had to procure himself.

> Exposed to the inclement skies,
> Deserted and forlorn he lies;
> No friend or fellow-mourner there,
> To soothe his sorrows and divide his care.

SOPHOCLES (Francklin's tr.)

Michael Clarke

Still enraged at their former ill-treatment of him, Philoctetes at first refused the request of the two chiefs. Their mission would have failed had not Hercules appeared to him in a dream and advised him to go to Troy, telling him that his wound would be healed by the famous Machaon. He then gladly went with Ulysses and Diomede. On his arrival at the Grecian camp the great physician cured him by casting him into a deep sleep and cutting away the diseased flesh from the injured foot. He awoke in perfect health and strength, and at once joined his countrymen in the war, resolved to make good use of his fatal arrows.

An opportunity soon offered, for the Trojans now began again to venture out in the open plain, thinking that the Greeks were not so dangerous since the terrible Achilles was no longer at their head. Their new general in chief was Paris, and Philoctetes, happening to encounter him in battle, aimed at him with one of his poisoned arrows and pierced him through the shoulder. Paris was immediately carried back to the city, suffering intense pain, for the poison quickly began to take effect. Then at last the thoughts of Paris turned to the fair Œnone, whom, twenty years before, he had left in sorrow and loneliness on Mount Ida. He remembered her words, that he would one day have recourse to her for help. Hoping, therefore, that she might take pity on him, and perhaps cure him of his wound, for she had been instructed in medicine by Apollo, he ordered his attendants to carry him to where she still dwelt on the slopes of Ida. Œnone had not forgotten his cruel desertion of her, and so she refused to use her skill in his behalf. But when she heard that he was dead, she came down to Troy, and in her grief threw herself on his funeral pyre, and perished by his side.

> She rose, and slowly down,
> By the long torrent's ever-deepen'd roar,
> Paced, following, as in trance, the silent cry.
> Then moving quickly forward till the heat

Smote on her brow, she lifted up a voice
Of shrill command, "Who burns upon the pyre?"
Whereon their oldest and their boldest said,
"He whom thou wouldst not heal!" and all at once
The morning light of happy marriage broke
Thro' all the clouded years of widowhood,
And muffling up her comely head, and crying
"Husband!" she leapt upon the funeral pile,
And mixt herself with him and past in fire.

TENNYSON, *Death of Œnone*.

Meanwhile the Ithacan king, not forgetting the other conditions mentioned by Helenus, set sail for the island of Scyros, where the son of Achilles resided. His name was Pyr'rhus, or Ne-op-tol'-mus, and, as he was a brave youth, he rejoiced at having an opportunity of fighting the Trojans, by whom his father had been killed. Ulysses gave him his father's armor, and by many heroic deeds in the war he proved that he was worthy to wear it.

The Palladium was now to be carried off from Troy, and this was a task by no means easy to perform. But the man of many arts succeeded in accomplishing it. Putting on the garments of a beggar, and scourging his body so as to leave marks, he went to the Scæan Gate, and entreated the guards to admit him. He told them that he was a Greek slave, and that he wished to escape from his master who had cruelly ill-used him. The guards, believing his story, permitted him to enter the city.

"He had given himself
Unseemly stripes, and o'er his shoulders flung
Vile garments like a slave's, and entered thus
The enemy's town, and walked its spacious streets.
Another man he seemed in that disguise.—
A beggar, though when at the Achaian fleet

Michael Clarke

So different was the semblance that he wore.
He entered Ilium thus transformed, and none
Knew who it was that passed."

BRYANT, *Odyssey*, Book IV.

But Helen, happening to pass by at a place near the king's palace, where the pretended beggar sat down to rest, immediately recognized him. He made a sign to her to keep silent, thinking that Paris being now dead, Helen perhaps was friendly to the Greeks, and wished them to take Troy, so that she might return to her own country. In this Ulysses was right, as very soon appeared, and as Helen declared years afterwards, when telling to his own son, Telemachus, the story of the Ithacan king's adventure within the walls of Troy.

"For I already longed
For my old home, and deeply I deplored
The evil fate that Venus brought on me,
Who led me thither from my own dear land."

BRYANT, *Odyssey*, Book IV.

Helen passed on without uttering a word, but in the evening she sent one of her maids to bring Ulysses secretly to her apartment in the palace. There she expressed her joy at meeting her countryman, and after hospitably entertaining him, she listened with pleasure to his plans. She then told him of the plans of the Trojans, and where and how the Palladium was to be got. Having thus obtained the information he desired, Ulysses contrived to make his way back unobserved to the Greek camp. In a few days he returned, accompanied by Diomede. They got into the city by scaling the walls, and Diomede, climbing on the shoulders of Ulysses, entered the citadel. Here, by following the directions given by Helen, he found the famous statue, and he and his companion carried it off to their friends at the ships, who rejoiced at the success of the undertaking.

Troy was now no longer under the protection of Pallas Minerva. Though that goddess helped the Greeks in their battles, she was obliged to save the city itself while it contained her sacred statue. But the Palladium being no longer within the walls, she was now at liberty to help the Greeks to capture and destroy the city. She therefore put into the mind of Ulysses the idea of the wooden horse, and she instructed the Greek chief E-pe'us how to make it. This horse was of vast size, large enough to contain about a hundred men, for it was hollow within.

> By Minerva's aid, a fabric reared,
> Which like a steed of monstrous height appeared;
> The sides were flanked with pine.
>
> VERGIL.

When it was finished, provisions were put into it. Then Ulysses, and Pyrrhus, and Menelaus, and Epeus, and a number of other Greek warriors, mounted into it by means of a ladder, after which the opening was fastened by strong bolts.

> In the hollow side,
> Selected numbers of their soldiers hide;
> With inward arms the dire machine they load;
> And iron bowels stuff the dark abode.
>
> VERGIL.

Meanwhile the other Greeks broke up their camp, and all going aboard their ships, they set sail, as if they had given up the siege, and were about to return to Greece. But they went no farther than the island of Ten'e-dos, about three miles

Michael Clarke

from the shore.

> In sight of Troy lies Tenedos, an isle
> (While Fortune did on Priam's empire smile)
> Renowned for wealth; but since, a faithless bay,
> Where ships exposed to wind and weather lay.
> There was their fleet concealed.

VERGIL.

As soon as the Trojans saw from their walls that the tents of the enemy were removed, and that their fleet had departed, they were filled with surprise and delight. They believed that the Greeks had given up the war, and so, throwing open their gates, they rushed out in multitudes upon the plain, King Priam riding in his chariot at their head.

> The Trojans, cooped within their walls so long,
> Unbar their gates, and issue in a throng
> Like swarming bees, and with delight survey
> The camp deserted, where the Grecians lay.

VERGIL.

But soon their attention was attracted by the huge wooden horse, and they gathered about it, astonished at its great size, and wondering what it meant. Some thought that it meant evil to Troy, and advised that it should be burned; others proposed that it should be hauled into the city and placed within the citadel. La-oc'o-on, one of Priam's sons, who was also a priest of Apollo, cried out in a loud voice, warning the king and people against doing this. "Are you so foolish," he exclaimed, "as to suppose that the enemy are gone? Put no faith in this horse. Whatever it is, I fear the Greeks even when offering gifts."

"This hollow fabric either must enclose
Within its blind recess, our secret foes;
Or 'tis an engine raised above the town
To overlook the walls, and then to batter down.
Somewhat is sure designed by fraud or force:
Trust not their presents, nor admit the horse."

VERGIL.

Thus saying, Laocoon hurled his spear against the side of the horse, and it sent forth a hollow sound like a deep groan. But at this moment a stranger, having the appearance of a Greek, was brought before the king. Some Trojan shepherds, finding him loitering on the river bank, had made him prisoner. Being asked who he was and why he was there, he told an artful story. His name, he said, was Si'non, and he was a Greek. His countrymen, having decided to give up the war, resolved to offer one of themselves as a sacrifice to the gods, that they might get fair winds to return home, and they selected him to be the victim. To escape that terrible fate he concealed himself among the reeds by the side of the Scamander until the fleet departed. This was Sinon's account of himself. The Trojans believed it, and the prisoner was set free. But the king asked him to tell them about the wooden horse,—why it had been made, and left there upon the plain.

Then Sinon told another false story. He said that the horse was a peace offering to Minerva, who had been angry because the Palladium was taken from Troy. For that insult to her, the goddess commanded the Greeks to return to their own country, and Calchas ordered them to build the horse as an atonement for their crime. He also told them to make it so large that the Trojans might not be able to drag it within their gates; for if it were brought into the city, it would be a protection to Troy, but if any harm were done to it, ruin would come on the kingdom of Priam.

"We raised and dedicate this wondrous frame,
So lofty, lest through your forbidden gates
It pass, and intercept our better fates;
For, once admitted there, our hopes are lost;
And Troy may then a new Palladium boast
For so religion and the gods ordain,
That, if you violate with hands profane
Minerva's gift, your town in flames shall burn;
(Which omen, O ye gods, on Græcia turn!)
But if it climb, with your assisting hands,
The Trojan walls, and in the city stands;
Then Troy shall Argos and Mycenæ burn,
And the reverse of fate on us return."

VERGIL.

King Priam and the Trojans believed this story too, and a
terrible thing which just then happened made them believe it
all the more. After Laocoon had hurled his spear at the
wooden horse, he and his two sons went to offer sacrifice to
the gods at an altar erected on the beach. While they were
thus engaged, two enormous serpents, darting out from the
sea, glided up to the altar, seized the priest and his sons, and
crushed all three to death in their tremendous coils.

First around the tender boys they wind,
Then with their sharpened fangs their limbs and bodies
grind.
The wretched father, running to their aid
With pious haste, but vain, they next invade:
Twice round his waist their winding volumes rolled;
And twice about his gasping throat they fold.
The priest thus doubly choked—their crests divide,
And towering o'er his head in triumph ride.

VERGIL.

The terrified Trojans regarded this awful event as a punishment sent by the gods upon Laocoon for insulting Minerva by casting his spear at her gift, which they now believed the horse to be. They therefore resolved to take the huge figure into the city in spite of the advice of Cassandra, who also warned them that it would bring ruin upon Troy. And so they made a great breach in the walls, for none of their gates were large enough to admit the vast image, and fastening strong ropes to its feet they dragged it into the citadel. Then they decorated the temples with garlands of green boughs, and spent the remainder of the day in festivity and rejoicing.

But in the dead of the night, when they were all sunk in deep repose, the treacherous Sinon drew the bolts from the trapdoor in the side of the wooden horse, and out came the Greek warriors, rejoicing at the success of their stratagem.

Sinon next hurried down to the beach, and there kindled a fire as a signal to his countrymen on the ships. They knew what it meant, for it was part of the plan that had been agreed on. Quickly plying their oars, they soon reached the shore, and, marching across the plain, the Greeks poured in thousands into the streets, through the breach that had been made in the walls.

The Trojans, startled from their sleep by the noise, understood at once what had happened. Hastily they rushed to arms, and, led and encouraged by Æneas and other chiefs, they fought valiantly to drive out the enemy, but all their valor was in vain. Troy was at last taken. The victorious Greeks swept through the city, dealing death and destruction around them. King Priam was slain by Pyrrhus, at the foot of the altar in one of the temples, to which he fled for safety. His son Deiphobus, who had married Helen after the death of Paris, was slain by Menelaus. The Spartan king, believing that what his wife had done had been decreed by the Fates

Michael Clarke

and the will of the gods, pardoned her and took her with him to his ships. The women of the Trojan royal family were carried off as slaves.

Æneas, with his father Anchises and his son I-u'lus, escaped from the city, and sailed from Troas with a fleet and a number of warlike followers. After many adventures by sea and land, which the Roman poet, Ver'gil, tells about in his poem called the Æ-ne'id, he reached Italy. There he established a settlement, and his descendants, it is said, were the founders of Rome.

Having completed their work of destruction and carried off to their ships all the riches of Troy, the Greeks set fire to the city, and in a few hours nothing remained but a mass of smouldering ruins. So ended the famous Trojan War. The prophecy of the soothsayer, Æsacus, at the birth of Paris, was fulfilled. Paris had brought destruction upon his family and country.

XIII. THE GREEK CHIEFS AFTER THE WAR

Great was the rejoicing of the Greeks at having at last brought the long and terrible war to a successful end. They had lost heavily in men and treasure, but they had defeated and destroyed the enemy, and taken possession of all the wealth of the rich city of Troy. They now looked forward with pleasure to the prospect of a safe return to their homes and families, which they had not seen for ten years. But for some of them, as we shall see, this happy hope was never realized.

The most unfortunate of them all was Agamemnon. He reached his kingdom and city of Mycenæ in safety, but he was there cruelly murdered by Æ-gis'thus, a relative of his, whom his wife, Clytemnestra, had married during his absence.

> Ægisthus planned a snare.
> He chose among the people twenty men,
> The bravest, whom he stationed out of sight,
> And gave command that others should prepare
> A banquet. Then with chariots and with steeds,
> And with a deadly purpose in his heart,
> He went, and, meeting Agamemnon, bade
> The shepherd of the people to the feast,
> And slew him at the board.

BRYANT, *Odyssey*, Book IV.

Michael Clarke

The Trojan princess, Cassandra, who accompanied Agamemnon to Mycenæ, had warned him of his doom, but as usual her words were disregarded, and she herself was slain at the same time as the ill-fated king. Agamemnon had a son named O-res'tes, who was then but a boy, and Ægisthus intended to kill him also, but the youth's sister, E-lec'tra, contrived to have him sent secretly to the court of his uncle, Stro'phi-us, king of Pho'cis. Here he was affectionately received and tenderly cared for. His constant companion was his cousin, Pyl'a-des, the son of Strophius, and so strong was their friendship for each other that it became famous in song and story.

When Orestes reached the years of manhood, he resolved to punish the murderers of his father. With this object he went to Mycenæ, taking with him his friend and companion, Pylades; and having obtained admission to the royal palace, he slew Ægisthus.

> Seven years in rich Mycenæ he bore rule,
> And on the eighth, to his destruction, came
> The nobly-born Orestes, just returned
> From Athens, and cut off that man of blood,
> The crafty wretch Ægisthus, by whose hand
> Fell his illustrious father.

BRYANT, *Odyssey*, Book III.

As Clytemnestra had taken part in the murder of Agamemnon, Orestes slew her also. This killing of his own mother provoked the anger of the gods, and Orestes was commanded to go to the oracle of Apollo, at Delphi, to learn there what punishment he should suffer for his crime. He obeyed, and the oracle told him that he must bring to Greece a statue of Diana which was then in the temple of that goddess in Taurica.

This was a dangerous enterprise, for the king of Taurica had a practice of sacrificing in that very temple any foreigners found in his country. Nevertheless Orestes undertook the task. He went to Taurica, accompanied, as usual, by his ever faithful friend Pylades. No sooner had they arrived than they were seized and carried before the king, and condemned to be sacrificed. But Orestes discovered, to his surprise and delight, that the priestess of the temple was his own sister, Iphigenia, who, as will be remembered, had been carried away many years before by Diana herself, when about to be sacrificed by the Greeks at Aulis. By the help of Iphigenia, the two friends not only escaped from Taurica, but carried off the statue, and Iphigenia returned with them to Greece. Orestes succeeded to the throne of his father, and as king of Mycenæ he lived and reigned many years in prosperity and happiness.

Menelaus returned to his kingdom of Sparta with his wife, Helen, but he had many wanderings and adventures. He was detained by unfavorable winds for some time on an island near the coast of Egypt, and he might never have reached home but for the advice he received from Pro'teus, one of the sea gods. It was no easy matter to get advice from Proteus. It was very difficult to find him, and still more difficult to get him to answer questions, for he had a habit of changing himself rapidly into many different forms, and so escaping from those who came to consult him. But Menelaus had the good fortune of meeting a water nymph named I-do'the-a, a daughter of Proteus, and she directed him what to do. There was a certain cave near the seaside, to which the Old Man of the Sea, as Proteus was sometimes called, came every day at noon to sleep. Idothea told Menelaus he would find the old man there, and that he must seize him quickly in his arms, and hold him fast in spite of all his changes, until he took the shape in which he had first appeared. Then he would answer any question put to him.

Michael Clarke

"As soon
As ye behold him stretched at length, exert
Your utmost strength to hold him there, although
He strive and struggle to escape your hands;
For he will try all stratagems, and take
The form of every reptile on the earth,
And turn to water and to raging flame,—
Yet hold him firmly still, and all the more
Make fast the bands. When he again shall take
The form in which thou sawest him asleep,
Desist from force, and loose the bands that held
The ancient prophet. Ask of him what god
Afflicts thee thus, and by what means to cross
The fishy deep and find thy home again."

BRYANT, *Odyssey*, Book IV.

Menelaus followed these directions, taking with him three of his bravest warriors, as Idothea also advised. They found Proteus, and rushing upon him, they seized and held him firmly in their grip, though he tried hard to escape.

First he took the shape
Of a maned lion, of a serpent next,
Then of a panther, then of a huge boar,
Then turned to flowing water, then became
A tall tree full of leaves. With resolute hearts
We held him fast, until the aged seer
Was weaned out, in spite of all his wiles.

BRYANT, *Odyssey*, Book IV,

The Old Man of the Sea then told Menelaus that he must go to Egypt, to the river there, and offer sacrifices to the gods, and that they would send him forth upon his voyage home, which would be speedy and safe. The Greek chief did as Proteus directed, and the prophecy was fulfilled. He soon reached his Spartan home, where, with his famous queen, Helen, he spent the remainder of his life in happiness.

Idomeneus, the warrior king of Crete, reached his island kingdom in safety.

> Idomeneus brought also back to Crete
> All his companions who survived the war;
> The sea took none of them.

BRYANT, *Odyssey*, Book III.

But a sad event occurred on his arrival in the island. During his voyage home there was a terrible storm, and Idomeneus much feared that his fleet might be destroyed. He then made a vow that if his ships escaped, he would sacrifice to Neptune the first living creature he met on landing. Unfortunately this happened to be his own son, who came down to the shore to receive and welcome his father. Idomeneus, though overwhelmed with grief, nevertheless fulfilled his promise to the god, but the Cre'tans were so incensed at the inhuman act that they banished him from the island.

> A flying rumor had been spread
> That fierce Idomeneus from Crete was fled,
> Expelled and exiled.

VERGIL.

Thus driven from his own country Idomeneus sailed westward until he came to the southern coast of Italy, where he founded the city and colony of Sal-len'tia, and lived to an extreme old age.

The fate of Ajax Oileus, king of Locris, was almost as terrible as that of Agamemnon. On the night of the destruction of Troy he had cruelly ill-treated the princess Cassandra, whom he dragged from the altar of the temple of Minerva, to which she had fled for refuge. Even the Greeks themselves were shocked at the crime, and they threatened to punish him for it. He was, however, allowed to set sail for Greece. But Minerva borrowed from Jupiter his flaming thunderbolts, and, obtaining permission from Neptune, she raised a furious tempest, which destroyed the Locrian king's ship. He himself swam to a rock, and as he sat there he defiantly cried out that he was safe in spite of all the gods. This insult to the immortals brought upon him the wrath of Neptune, who, smiting the rock with his awful trident, hurled the impious Ajax into the depths of the sea.

He had said
That he, in spite of all the gods, would come
Safe from those mountain waves. When Neptune heard
The boaster's challenge, instantly he laid
His strong hand on the trident, smote the rock
And cleft it to the base. Part stood erect,
Part fell into the deep. There Ajax sat,
And felt the shock, and with the falling mass
Was carried headlong to the billowy depths
Below, and drank the brine and perished there.

BRYANT, *Odyssey*, Book IV.

The venerable Nestor reached his home without misfortune or accident He ended his days in peace in his kingdom of Pylos, though he had to mourn the loss of his brave son Antilochus, whom Memnon had slain.

Diomede also reached his kingdom of Ætolia, but he found that in his absence his home had been seized by a stranger. This was a punishment sent upon him by Venus, whom, as we have seen, he had wounded in the hand at the siege of Troy.

"Mad as I was, when I, with mortal arms,
Presumed against immortal powers to move,
And violate with wounds the queen of love."

VERGIL.

Quitting his kingdom and country, the warrior wandered to other lands. He finally settled in the south of Italy, where he built a city, which he called Ar-gyr'i-pa, and married the daughter of Dau'nus, the king of the country.

Great Diomede has compassed round with walls
The city, which Argyripa he calls,
From his own Argos named.

VERGIL.

Neoptolemus, or Pyrrhus, the son of Achilles, returned to Phthia, where his grandfather, Peleus, still lived and reigned. He took with him Andromache and Helenus, the only one of Priam's sons who lived after the destruction of Troy. Pyrrhus, died a few years after his return, and Andromache became the wife of Helenus. The Trojan prince soon gained the friendship of Peleus, who gave him a kingdom in E-pi'rus to rule over, and here he and Andromache spent the remainder of their lives together.

But no one of all the warrior chiefs of Greece who fought at Troy met with so many dangers in returning to his native land as the famous Ulysses. Ten year elapsed after the end of the great war before he reached his Ithacan home. There he was welcomed by his devoted wife, Penelope, and his affectionate son, Telemachus, who had passed all those years in loving remembrance of him and anxious hope of his coming. His wonderful adventures during his many wanderings are described in Homer's Odyssey. An account of them would fill another book like this Story of Troy.

Michael Clarke

PERSONS AND PLACES MENTIONED

Ac' a mas
A cha'ians
(yans)
A chil'les
Æ ge'an
Æ gis'thus
Æ ne'as
Æ ne'id
Æs' a cus
Æs cu la' pi us
Æt'na
Æ to' li a
Ag a mem' non
A ge'nor
A'jax
Am'a zons
An drom'ache
An te' nor
An til'o chus
An'ti phus
Aph ro di' te
A pol' lo
Ar che la' us
Ar chil'o chus
Ar'gives
Ar'gos

Ar gyr' i pa
As ty'a nax
A'treus (trus)
A tri' des
At' ro pos
Au' lis
Au ro'ra
Au tom' e don
Bac'chus
Ba' li us
Bo' re as
Bri'a reus (rus)
Bri se' is
Cal'chas
Cal li'o pe
Ca'ri a
Cas san'dra
Cas ta' li a
Ce lu'o nes
Chi' ron
Chry se' is
Chry'ses
Clo' tho
Clyt em nes'
tra
Co'on

Cran'a ë
Cres'si da
Cre'tans
Cy'clops
Dar da nelles'
Dar da' ni a
Dar' da nus
Dau' nus
De iph' o bus
Del' phi
Di an' a
Di' o mede
Di' o ne
Dis cor' di a
Do' lon
E ë' ti on
E'gypt
E lec' tra
E pe' us
Eph i al' tes
E pi' rus
E' ris
E thi o' pi a
Eu phor' bus
Eu ryl' a tes
Eu ryn' o me

Gan' y mede
Glau' cus
Ha' des
Hec' tor
Hec' u ba
Hel' e nus
Hel' las
He~r' cu les
He~r' mes
He si' o ne
Ho' mer
I dæ' us
I dom' e neus
(nus)
I do' the a
Il' i on
Il' i um
I' lus
I phid' a mas
Iph i ge ni' a
I' ris I' sus
Ith' a ca
I u' lus
Ju' no
Ju' pi ter
Lach' e sis
La e~r' tes
La oc' o ön
La od a mi' a
La od' i çe
La od' o cus
La om' e don
La to' na
Le' da
Lem' nos
Le~r' na
Les' bos

Lo' cris
Lyc' i a
Lyc o me' des
Lyr nes' sus
Ma cha' on
Me' les
Mel e sig' e nes
Mem' non
Men e la' us
Me~r' cu ry
Me ri' o nes
Mi ne~r' va
My çe' næ
Myr' mi dons
Mys' i a
Ne op tol' e
mus
Nep' tune
Ne re' i des
Ne' re us
Nes' tor
O dys' seus
(sus) Œ no' ne
O i' leus (lus)
O lym' pus
O res' tes
O' tus
Pæ' on
Pal a me' des
Pal la' di um
Pal' las
Pan' da rus
Par nas' sus
Par' is
Par' the non
Pa tro' clus
Ped' a sus

Pe leus (lus)
Pe' li on
Pel o pon ne'
sus
Pe' lops
Pe nel' o pe
Pen the si le' a
Pe~r' ga mus
Pher' e clus
Phil oc te' tes
Pho' çis
Phœ' bus
Phœ' nix
Phryg' i a
Phthi' a
Phyl' a ce
Plu' to
Po dar' ces
Po lyd' a mas
Pol y do' rus
Pri' am
Pro tes i la' us
Pro' teus (tus)
Pyl' a des
Py⁻' los
Pyr' rhus
Pyth' i a
Rhe' sus
Sal' a mis
Sal len' tia
Sam' o thrace
Sar pe' don
Sca man' der
Sca man' dri us
Sçy⁻' ros
Siç' i ly
Sim' o is

Michael Clarke

Si' non

Smin'theus

(thus)

Smyr' na

So'cus

Som' nus

Spar' ta

Sten' tor

Sthen' e lus

Stro' phi us

Tal thyb' i us

Tar' ta rus

Tau' ri ca

Tel' a mon

Te lem' achus

Tel' e phus

Ten' e dos

Teu' cer

Teu' cri a

Teu thra' ni a

The' be

The~r si' tes

Thes' sa ly

The' tis

Ti tho' nus

Tro' as

Tro' ilus

Ty¯' deus (dus)

Ty di¯' des

Tyn' da rus

U lys' ses

Ve' nus

Ver' gil

Vul' can

Xan' thus

Zeph' y rus

Choose from Thousands of 1stWorldLibrary Classics By

A. M. Barnard
Ada Leverson
Adolphus William Ward
Aesop
Agatha Christie
Alexander Aaronsohn
Alexander Kielland
Alexandre Dumas
Alfred Gatty
Alfred Ollivant
Alice Duer Miller
Alice Turner Curtis
Alice Dunbar
Allen Chapman
Alleyne Ireland
Ambrose Bierce
Amelia E. Barr
Amory H. Bradford
Andrew Lang
Andrew McFarland Davis
Andy Adams
Angela Brazil
Anna Alice Chapin
Anna Sewell
Annie Besant
Annie Hamilton Donnell
Annie Payson Call
Annie Roe Carr
Annonaymous
Anton Chekhov
Archibald Lee Fletcher
Arnold Bennett
Arthur C. Benson
Arthur Conan Doyle
Arthur M. Winfield
Arthur Ransome
Arthur Schnitzler
Arthur Train
Atticus
B.H. Baden-Powell
B. M. Bower
B. C. Chatterjee
Baroness Emmuska Orczy
Baroness Orczy
Basil King
Bayard Taylor
Ben Macomber
Bertha Muzzy Bower
Bjornstjerne Bjornson

Booth Tarkington
Boyd Cable
Bram Stoker
C. Collodi
C. E. Orr
C. M. Ingleby
Carolyn Wells
Catherine Parr Traill
Charles A. Eastman
Charles Amory Beach
Charles Dickens
Charles Dudley Warner
Charles Farrar Browne
Charles Ives
Charles Kingsley
Charles Klein
Charles Hanson Towne
Charles Lathrop Pack
Charles Romyn Dake
Charles Whibley
Charles Willing Beale
Charlotte M. Braeme
Charlotte M. Yonge
Charlotte Perkins Stetson
Clair W. Hayes
Clarence Day Jr.
Clarence E. Mulford
Clemence Housman
Confucius
Coningsby Dawson
Cornelis DeWitt Wilcox
Cyril Burleigh
D. H. Lawrence
Daniel Defoe
David Garnett
Dinah Craik
Don Carlos Janes
Donald Keyhoe
Dorothy Kilner
Dougan Clark
Douglas Fairbanks
E. Nesbit
E. P. Roe
E. Phillips Oppenheim
E. S. Brooks
Earl Barnes
Edgar Rice Burroughs
Edith Van Dyne
Edith Wharton

Edward Everett Hale
Edward J. O'Biren
Edward S. Ellis
Edwin L. Arnold
Eleanor Atkins
Eleanor Hallowell Abbott
Eliot Gregory
Elizabeth Gaskell
Elizabeth McCracken
Elizabeth Von Arnim
Ellem Key
Emerson Hough
Emilie F. Carlen
Emily Bronte
Emily Dickinson
Enid Bagnold
Enilor Macartney Lane
Erasmus W. Jones
Ernie Howard Pie
Ethel May Dell
Ethel Turner
Ethel Watts Mumford
Eugene Sue
Eugenie Foa
Eugene Wood
Eustace Hale Ball
Evelyn Everett-green
Everard Cotes
F. H. Cheley
F. J. Cross
F. Marion Crawford
Fannie E. Newberry
Federick Austin Ogg
Ferdinand Ossendowski
Fergus Hume
Florence A. Kilpatrick
Fremont B. Deering
Francis Bacon
Francis Darwin
Frances Hodgson Burnett
Frances Parkinson Keyes
Frank Gee Patchin
Frank Harris
Frank Jewett Mather
Frank L. Packard
Frank V. Webster
Frederic Stewart Isham
Frederick Trevor Hill
Frederick Winslow Taylor

Friedrich Kerst
Friedrich Nietzsche
Fyodor Dostoyevsky
G.A. Henty
G.K. Chesterton
Gabrielle E. Jackson
Garrett P. Serviss
Gaston Leroux
George A. Warren
George Ade
Geroge Bernard Shaw
George Cary Eggleston
George Durston
George Ebers
George Eliot
George Gissing
George MacDonald
George Meredith
George Orwell
George Sylvester Viereck
George Tucker
George W. Cable
George Wharton James
Gertrude Atherton
Gordon Casserly
Grace E. King
Grace Gallatin
Grace Greenwood
Grant Allen
Guillermo A. Sherwell
Gulielma Zollinger
Gustav Flaubert
H. A. Cody
H. B. Irving
H.C. Bailey
H. G. Wells
H. H. Munro
H. Irving Hancock
H. R. Naylor
H. Rider Haggard
H. W. C. Davis
Haldeman Julius
Hall Caine
Hamilton Wright Mabie
Hans Christian Andersen
Harold Avery
Harold McGrath
Harriet Beecher Stowe
Harry Castlemon
Harry Coghill
Harry Houidini

Hayden Carruth
Helent Hunt Jackson
Helen Nicolay
Hendrik Conscience
Hendy David Thoreau
Henri Barbusse
Henrik Ibsen
Henry Adams
Henry Ford
Henry Frost
Henry James
Henry Jones Ford
Henry Seton Merriman
Henry W Longfellow
Herbert A. Giles
Herbert Carter
Herbert N. Casson
Herman Hesse
Hildegard G. Frey
Homer
Honore De Balzac
Horace B. Day
Horace Walpole
Horatio Alger Jr.
Howard Pyle
Howard R. Garis
Hugh Lofting
Hugh Walpole
Humphry Ward
Ian Maclaren
Inez Haynes Gillmore
Irving Bacheller
Isabel Cecilia Williams
Isabel Hornibrook
Israel Abrahams
Ivan Turgenev
J.G.Austin
J. Henri Fabre
J. M. Barrie
J. M. Walsh
J. Macdonald Oxley
J. R. Miller
J. S. Fletcher
J. S. Knowles
J. Storer Clouston
J. W. Duffield
Jack London
Jacob Abbott
James Allen
James Andrews
James Baldwin

James Branch Cabell
James DeMille
James Joyce
James Lane Allen
James Lane Allen
James Oliver Curwood
James Oppenheim
James Otis
James R. Driscoll
Jane Abbott
Jane Austen
Jane L. Stewart
Janet Aldridge
Jens Peter Jacobsen
Jerome K. Jerome
Jessie Graham Flower
John Buchan
John Burroughs
John Cournos
John F. Kennedy
John Gay
John Glasworthy
John Habberton
John Joy Bell
John Kendrick Bangs
John Milton
John Philip Sousa
John Taintor Foote
Jonas Lauritz Idemil Lie
Jonathan Swift
Joseph A. Altsheler
Joseph Carey
Joseph Conrad
Joseph E. Badger Jr
Joseph Hergesheimer
Joseph Jacobs
Jules Vernes
Julian Hawthrone
Julie A Lippmann
Justin Huntly McCarthy
Kakuzo Okakura
Karle Wilson Baker
Kate Chopin
Kenneth Grahame
Kenneth McGaffey
Kate Langley Bosher
Kate Langley Bosher
Katherine Cecil Thurston
Katherine Stokes
L. A. Abbot
L. T. Meade

L. Frank Baum
Latta Griswold
Laura Dent Crane
Laura Lee Hope
Laurence Housman
Lawrence Beasley
Leo Tolstoy
Leonid Andreyev
Lewis Carroll
Lewis Sperry Chafer
Lilian Bell
Lloyd Osbourne
Louis Hughes
Louis Joseph Vance
Louis Tracy
Louisa May Alcott
Lucy Fitch Perkins
Lucy Maud Montgomery
Luther Benson
Lydia Miller Middleton
Lyndon Orr
M. Corvus
M. H. Adams
Margaret E. Sangster
Margret Howth
Margaret Vandercook
Margaret W. Hungerford
Margret Penrose
Maria Edgeworth
Maria Thompson Daviess
Mariano Azuela
Marion Polk Angellotti
Mark Overton
Mark Twain
Mary Austin
Mary Catherine Crowley
Mary Cole
Mary Hastings Bradley
Mary Roberts Rinehart
Mary Rowlandson
M. Wollstonecraft Shelley
Maud Lindsay
Max Beerbohm
Myra Kelly
Nathaniel Hawthrone
Nicolo Machiavelli
O. F. Walton
Oscar Wilde

Owen Johnson
P.G. Wodehouse
Paul and Mabel Thorne
Paul G. Tomlinson
Paul Severing
Percy Brebner
Percy Keese Fitzhugh
Peter B. Kyne
Plato
Quincy Allen
R. Derby Holmes
R. L. Stevenson
R. S. Ball
Rabindranath Tagore
Rahul Alvares
Ralph Bonehill
Ralph Henry Barbour
Ralph Victor
Ralph Waldo Emmerson
Rene Descartes
Ray Cummings
Rex Beach
Rex E. Beach
Richard Harding Davis
Richard Jefferies
Richard Le Gallienne
Robert Barr
Robert Frost
Robert Gordon Anderson
Robert L. Drake
Robert Lansing
Robert Lynd
Robert Michael Ballantyne
Robert W. Chambers
Rosa Nouchette Carey
Rudyard Kipling
Saint Augustine
Samuel B. Allison
Samuel Hopkins Adams
Sarah Bernhardt
Sarah C. Hallowell
Selma Lagerlof
Sherwood Anderson
Sigmund Freud
Standish O'Grady
Stanley Weyman
Stella Benson
Stella M. Francis

Stephen Crane
Stewart Edward White
Stijn Streuvels
Swami Abhedananda
Swami Parmananda
T. S. Ackland
T. S. Arthur
The Princess Der Ling
Thomas A. Janvier
Thomas A Kempis
Thomas Anderton
Thomas Bailey Aldrich
Thomas Bulfinch
Thomas De Quincey
Thomas Dixon
Thomas H. Huxley
Thomas Hardy
Thomas More
Thornton W. Burgess
U. S. Grant
Upton Sinclair
Valentine Williams
Various Authors
Vaughan Kester
Victor Appleton
Victor G. Durham
Victoria Cross
Virginia Woolf
Wadsworth Camp
Walter Camp
Walter Scott
Washington Irving
Wilbur Lawton
Wilkie Collins
Willa Cather
Willard F. Baker
William Dean Howells
William le Queux
W. Makepeace Thackeray
William W. Walter
William Shakespeare
Winston Churchill
Yei Theodora Ozaki
Yogi Ramacharaka
Young E. Allison
Zane Grey

www.ingramcontent.com/pod-product-compliance
Lightning Source LLC
Chambersburg PA
CBHW021008180626
46814CB00003B/1186